What's Cooking, Uncle Sam?

The Government's Effect on the American Diet

WHAT'S COOKING, UNCLE SAM?
THE GOVERNMENT'S EFFECT ON THE AMERICAN DIET

By Alice D. Kamps

With a message from
David S. Ferriero
Archivist of the United States

Foreword by **José Andrés**

The Foundation for the National Archives
Washington, DC

What's Cooking, Uncle Sam?
The Government's Effect on the American Diet

Copyright ©2011
The Foundation for the National Archives
Washington, DC

This book is based on the exhibition "What's Cooking, Uncle Sam? The Government's Effect on the American Diet," presented in the Lawrence F. O'Brien Gallery at the National Archives Building, Washington, DC, from June 10, 2011, to January 3, 2012.

Written by Alice D. Kamps
Designed by Amanda Perez
Edited by Patty Reinert Mason
Copyedited by Benjamin Guterman

For the Foundation for the National Archives
Thora Colot, Executive Director
Patty Reinert Mason, Director of Publications
Kathleen Lietzau, Publications and Research Assistant

For the National Archives and Records Administration
Marvin Pinkert, Director, Center for the National Archives Experience
Christina Rudy Smith, Director of Exhibits
Alice D. Kamps, Curator
Amanda Perez, Designer
Benjamin Guterman, Copyeditor

Library of Congress Cataloging-in-Publication Data

Kamps, Alice D., 1963-
  What's cooking, Uncle Sam? : the government's effect on the American diet / by Alice D. Kamps ; with a message from David S. Ferriero ; foreword by Jose Andres.
       p. cm.
  Includes bibliographical references.
  Summary: "What's Cooking, Uncle Sam?, based on an exhibition at the National Archives in Washington, DC, is a collection of records exploring the history of food policy in the United States"-- Provided by publisher.
  ISBN 978-0-9841033-3-1 (hardcover) -- ISBN 978-0-9841033-4-8 (softcover)
  1. Nutrition policy--United States--Exhibitions. 2. Public records--United States--Exhibitions. 3. Diet--United States--Exhibitions. 4. United States. National Archives and Records Administration--Exhibitions. I. Title.
  TX360.U6K36 2011
  641.5'636--dc22
                          2011015976

ISBN (softcover): 978-0-9841033-4-8
ISBN (hardcover): 978-0-9841033-3-1

First published in 2011 by the Foundation for the National Archives
700 Pennsylvania Avenue NW, Room G12
Washington, DC 20408
www.nara.gov/nae/support

Printed in the United States by Todd Allan Printing

Front cover: "Get Your Farm in the Fight!" a 1942 poster from the U.S. Agriculture Department, encouraging farmers to increase food production in support of the war effort. Image adapted. See page 33. *Back cover:* "Know Your Onions" poster, ca. 1942. Image adapted. See page 73.

Photographic Credits
The majority of items reproduced in this book are from the holdings of the National Archives, which supplied the photographs, unless otherwise noted.

Front cover, p. 33, 44-PA-871-A; p. 2, 412-DA-1553; p. 6, *http://www.flickr.com/photos/whitehouse/3630249732*, accessed Apr. 4, 2011; pp. 8–9, 66–69, Records of the Agricultural Marketing Service, RG 136; pp. 11, 72, 4-P-127; p. 12, 44-PA-219; p. 15, 306-PSD-66-0789; p. 17, 54-FS-44572; p. 18, 54-FS-5624; p. 19 (top), 54-FS-5600; p. 19 (bottom), 54-FS-39136; pp. 20–21, Records of the Bureau of Plant Industry, Soils, and Agricultural Engineering, RG 54; p. 23, 16-EX-9-27339-C; p. 24, 33-SC-14524c; p. 25 (top), 16-EX-1-1; p. 25 (bottom), 33-A-93-5; p. 27, Records of the Office of Price Administration, RG 188; pp. 28, 29 (top), Records of the Bureau of Prisons, RG 129; p. 29 (bottom), Records of the U.S. House of Representatives, RG 233; p. 30, 83-G-44179; pp. 31, 41, Records of the Office of the Secretary of Agriculture, RG 16; p. 32 (left), 44-PA-919; p. 32 (right), 44-PA-2525; p. 35, 88-GB-6-LS-C-1599; p. 36, FDA History Office; p. 37, Records of the Bureau of Agricultural and Industrial Chemistry, RG 97; p. 38, Records of the Food and Drug Administration, RG 88; p. 39, DC Public Library; p. 40, General Records of the Department of State, RG 59; pp. 42, 58, 59, Records of the Patent and Trademark Office, RG 241; p. 43, 88-GP-23-C280; p. 44, 88-GB-2-C-1733; p. 45, 88-GB-2-C-342; p. 46, 17-PE-16; p. 47, 17-PE-3; p. 48, 88-GN-B-254; p. 49, General Records of the U.S. Government, RG 11; p. 51, 176-HE-33321-C; p. 52, 176-HE-24272-C; p. 53, 176-HE 24267-C; p. 55, Records of the Office of Education, RG 12; p. 56 (top), 462-CNP-1; pp. 53 (bottom), 63 (top), Publications of the U.S. Government, RG 287; p. 57, 44-PA-798B; p. 60, 176-HE-22912-C; p. 61, 176-HE-33254-C; p. 62, 16-G-168-S-22108C; p. 63 (bottom), 33-A-90-1; p. 64, 4-P-68; p. 65, NRE-4-IOWA-1; p. 70, 4-P-103; p. 71, 4-P-144; p. 73 (top), back cover, 44-PA-1230; p. 73 (bottom), 44-PA-998T; p. 74, 287-P-A1.32:G16; p. 75, 44-PA-216; p. 76, Franklin D. Roosevelt Presidential Library and Museum; p. 77, 208-AA-322I(2); p. 79, 111-SC-158424; p. 80, 44-PA-2562; p. 81, Records of Naval Districts and Shore Establishments, RG 181; p. 82, Records of the Office of the Quartermaster General, RG 92; p. 83, Records of the Veterans Administration, RG 15; p. 84, 44-PA-2242; p. 85, 44-PA-2290; p. 86, NWDNS-210-G-A72; p. 87, 44-PA-745; p. 88, NLRN-WHPO-E3367C-04A; p. 89, C315-2; pp. 90–91, Lyndon Baines Johnson Presidential Library and Museum; pp. 92 (left), 93, John F. Kennedy Presidential Library and Museum; p. 92 (right), Jimmy Carter Presidential Library and Museum; pp. 94–95, Dwight D. Eisenhower Presidential Library and Museum.

TABLE OF CONTENTS

Children from Bancroft Elementary School help First Lady Michelle Obama plant the White House Vegetable Garden, April 9, 2009.

Official White House Photo by Samantha Appleton

MESSAGE FROM THE ARCHIVIST OF THE UNITED STATES
DAVID S. FERRIERO

As Archivist of the United States, an important part of my job is to increase the public's interest in, and access to, the billions of Federal Government records we hold in trust for the American people. In the case of the records and photographs in the National Archives Experience's latest exhibition, "What's Cooking, Uncle Sam?" my job is easy. There are few topics that generate more enthusiasm in today's society than everybody's favorite subject: Food.

In "What's Cooking, Uncle Sam?" visitors to the National Archives will learn how the Government throughout our history has played an important role in ensuring that the food we eat is safe, nutritious, economical, and plentiful. The records in this exhibition demonstrate that many of our contemporary concerns about food—the diversity of crops, the benefits of eating locally grown foods, the debate over chemical additives, the resurging interest in school and community gardening—have been explored by generations before us.

But this fascinating exhibition is not just a collection of stories about food and government regulation. It also tells stories of bravery, and details the hardships endured by early agricultural explorers who scoured the earth for plant specimens and seeds to bring to America. It teaches us about chemist Harvey Wiley, the first commissioner of the U.S. Food and Drug Administration, who proved the harmful effects of chemical preservatives in food by testing them on humans.

The exhibition also includes records about home economics and about the role of women in our society. At a time in our history when few women pursued careers as scientists, many applied scientific research to their own kitchens, aiding the effort to protect the food supply while providing nutritious meals for their families. Records of school lunch and military food programs show us how American tastes were influenced by what the Government chose to serve at schools and on the battlefield. And finally, records from the Presidential libraries and museums provide a glimpse into the glamour and cuisine of the White House and show how our leaders influence our culinary traditions.

I hope this incredible exhibition, and the stories and images in this accompanying catalog, will give you a taste of the records available at the National Archives. I invite you to return, not only as a tourist, but as a researcher, to explore further.

FOREWORD
CHEF JOSÉ ANDRÉS

Eating is the one thing, besides breathing, that we all do from the day we are born until the day we die. And today, as in earlier times, it is critical to recognize that food—how we produce it, process it, package it, sell it, cook it, and eat it—is as important as any other issue, vitally connected to everything from culture to energy, art, science, the economy, national security, the environment, and health.

Our national Government has influenced the way we eat in America since the Revolutionary War, even while its role has been continually debated. Exploring that history, the National Archives Experience has put together a fascinating exhibition drawing attention to the importance of our food. "What's Cooking, Uncle Sam? The Government's Effect on the American Diet" is an astonishing look at America's history with the food we produce, package, and prepare for our families.

When I learned of this amazing exhibition at the National Archives, I had to be a part of it. As its Chief Culinary Advisor, I don't just speak for me; I speak on behalf of a long chain of individuals who work hard to feed people. Farmers, beekeepers, bakers, scientists, fishermen, grocers—we are all part of that chain, all food people, all dedicated to feeding our communities, our nation, our world. We work tirelessly to address the food issues in America, from obesity and nutrition to family farms and sustainable resources.

And having spent many years running my restaurants right near the National Archives, I also know the power that the Archives and its countless letters, posters, documents, and photographs have in telling the story of America. I am an immigrant from Spain, but Washington, DC, is my home, and the people of America are my family. I have walked the halls and exhibitions of the National Archives for years, learning the history of this amazing country that I now call my own.

"What's Cooking, Uncle Sam?" is such an exciting story to be a part of. The beloved institution that watches over our most important records now turns its attention to the world of food and the role that government plays—issues that are an important part of my life and those around me. My team and I have been so inspired by what the Archives has built with this exhibition and its focus on the Farm, the Factory, the Kitchen, and the Table, that we decided to bring it to life with a special dining destination.

Just steps away from the National Archives, we have created America Eats, a restaurant named after the Work Projects Administration's Federal Writers' Project, which documented the food traditions of the nation in the 1930s. A partnership with the Foundation for the National Archives, America Eats offers a modern interpretation of traditional American recipes and welcomes guests to explore the exhibition and experience a new way of looking at our history—on the plate!

I encourage everyone to start seeing food as the solution. Looking back through America's history in the fascinating artifacts of this exhibition, you see the lessons that have been learned and the issues we still face today. There will always be controversy and debate, but food is powerful in its reach. Every issue has different sides, but we have to see beyond the disagreements to look for common ground so that we can improve the way we feed America.

All of us are part of that discussion about food in America: chef and fast-food executive, small farmer and agribusiness, government and citizen. And not just America: what we do here has repercussions around the world. Food is also part of foreign policy; food is national security; food is energy policy.

Children come to the Archives every day to see the records connected to the founding of this country. This exhibition allows us to plant a little seed, to get youngsters interested in food matters today and create big changes in the future. Food used the right way can end hunger and help fight obesity and malnutrition. Food and the right farming practices will create employment and prosperity. Food when wholesomely grown and prepared can help improve the environment.

Food can be the answer.

About Chef José Andrés
José Andrés, Chief Culinary Advisor to "What's Cooking, Uncle Sam?" is the award-winning chef, owner, and creative force behind ThinkFoodGroup with 10 restaurants across the United States. An internationally acclaimed broadcaster and author, Andrés is a passionate advocate for advancing food policy in America and the developing world.

Acknowledgments

I feel a very unusual sensation—if it is not indigestion, I think it must be gratitude.
—Benjamin Disraeli

With research in more than a hundred original records and dozens of photographs, the National Archives Experience's 2011 exhibition "What's Cooking, Uncle Sam?" required the efforts, knowledge, and skills of many individuals. First and foremost, I would like to thank Christina Rudy Smith, Director of Exhibits at the National Archives Experience, who conceived the exhibit and gave me the opportunity to curate it.

The exhibition was created under the direction of Marvin Pinkert, Director of the Center for the National Archives Experience. James Zeender, Karen Hibbitt, Alexis Hill, and Patrick Kepley served as exhibit registrars. Ray Ruskin designed the exhibition; Amanda Perez designed the exhibit graphics and this catalog. Thomas Nastick and Darlene McClurkin produced the exhibit videos. Maureen MacDonald copyedited the exhibit text, and Benjamin Guterman copyedited the catalog text. Other colleagues at the National Archives Experience—Will Sandoval, Jennifer Johnson, Bruce Bustard, and Catherine Farmer—helped me to navigate the records, hallways, and procedures of the National Archives.

I'm grateful to Archivist of the United States David S. Ferriero and Chef José Andrés for their support of the exhibition and their contributions to this book.

The Foundation for the National Archives, under the direction of Thora Colot, generously supported the exhibition and published this catalog. Director of Publications Patty Reinert Mason managed the project and edited the book, while Publications and Research Assistant Kathleen Lietzau provided valuable administrative and editing support. I would also like to thank Director of Development Stefanie Mathew, who led the fundraising effort for the exhibition and was instrumental in forming our partnership with Chef Andrés and the ThinkFoodGroup, and Director of Administration and Marketing Franck Cordes, who led the marketing effort.

In addition, I am grateful to the following National Archives staff for their expertise and assistance: Holly Reed, Ed McCarter, Rutha Beamon, Mary Ilario, Vernon Early, and Mark Meader from the Special Media Archives Services; Jeffrey Reed, Jennifer Seitz, and Michelle Farnsworth from Special Media Preservation; Terry Boone, Ann Wilker, Susan Page, Sarah Raithel, Lisa Hall Isbell, Steven Loew, Lauren Varga, Sara Shpargel, Kathleen Ludwig, Jana Dambrogio, and Daniel Dancis from Document Conservation; Jane Fitzgerald, Patricia

Anderson, Victor Johnson, and Jacqueline Budell from Textual Archives Services; Suzanne Isaacs from Policy and Planning; Susan Cooper, Miriam Kleiman, and Laura Diachenko from Public Affairs and Communications; Rebecca Martin from Volunteer Services; and Christine Blackerby, Jessica Kratz, Andrew McCabe, and Garret Szanther from the Center for Legislative Archives.

The assistance of a number of dedicated individuals at the Presidential libraries and Regional Archives was invaluable: Alycia Vivona at the Franklin D. Roosevelt Presidential Library and Museum; Michael MacDonald, Renee Bair, Barbara Cline, and Margaret Harman at the Lyndon Baines Johnson Library and Museum; Melissa Walker, Christine Mouw, and John Keller at the William J. Clinton Presidential Library and Museum; Sara Saunders, David Stanhope, Mary Ann McSweeney, and Sylvia Naguib at the Jimmy Carter Library and Museum; James Draper, David Horrocks, and Donna Lehman at the Gerald R. Ford Presidential Library and Museum; Karen Abramson and Maryrose Grossman at the John F. Kennedy Presidential Library and Museum; Michelle Kopfer, Timothy Rives, Nathan Myers, Kathy Struss, and Deanna Kolling at the Dwight D. Eisenhower Presidential Library and Museum; Michael Pinckney at the Ronald Reagan Presidential Library; Olivia Anastasiadis, Christine Mickey, Tim Naftali, Melissa Lew Heddon, and Jason Schultz at the Nixon Presidential Library and Museum; James McSweeney and Robert G. Richards at the National Archives at Atlanta; and Scott Forsythe at the National Archives at Chicago.

In addition, three knowledgeable and generous historians—Douglas Helms at the U.S. Department of Agriculture, Suzanne Junod at the Food and Drug Administration History Office, and Harvey Levenstein at McMaster University in Hamilton, Ontario—reviewed the script and provided advice and encouragement. Susan Fugate, Dan Lech, Perry Ma, and Ellen Mann at the National Agricultural Library generously shared items from their collection; Greg Marcangelo at the Library of Congress, Faye Haskins at the Washingtoniana Division of the District of Columbia Public Library, and Cynthia Lachin at the Food and Drug Administration History Office helped secure images from their collections.

Finally, I would like to thank my husband, Mark Sandy, for his love and support.

Many thanks to you all.

Alice D. Kamps

Curator

INTRODUCTION

What's Cooking, Uncle Sam? is based on an exhibition at the National Archives' Lawrence F. O'Brien Gallery in Washington, DC. The exhibition is an eclectic assortment of records from the National Archives of the United States with one thing in common: they were produced in the course of government efforts to ensure that Americans enjoy an ample, safe, and nutritious diet. Spanning the Revolutionary War to the late 1900s, these records echo many of our current concerns about government's role in the health and safety of our food supply.

What's Cooking? explores four areas of government intervention: Farm, Factory, Kitchen, and Table. Sometimes the impact was significant: the Pure Food and Drugs Act of 1906 made it illegal to sell products doctored with toxic chemicals. Sometimes the impact was less dramatic: President Lyndon B. Johnson's Pedernales River Chili recipe spiced up the cooking repertoire of some of his fans. Sometimes there was little or no impact, despite the Government's best efforts: the World War II nutrition campaign had negligible effect on eating habits. And sometimes the impact was completely unintended: many children of immigrant parents came to prefer white bread after eating school lunch. The stories related here provide context and insight into today's conversation about the role of government in our daily diet.

The individuals engaged in government activities designed to regulate the food supply, understand nutrition, and educate the public produced a multitude of fascinating letters, legislation, photographs, pamphlets, posters, films, and radio programs. These records tell the story of battles against tainted ketchup, inferior tea, and oleomargarine; they allow us to hear the desperate voices of Depression-era farmers; and they explain how the Government got into the business of publishing recipes for cottage cheese loaf and teaching housewives to can peaches.

The opportunity to explore food records spanning two centuries provides insight into America's complex and conflicted relationship with food. From the farm to the dinner table, the records of the National Archives reveal the subtle and not-so-subtle ways that government has affected what Americans eat.

FARM

From local 4-H programs to omnibus farm bills, a wide variety of government activities influence what American farmers grow, how they grow it, and how much they earn selling it. As a major industry in the United States, agriculture has naturally been closely monitored by the Government. The number of Americans living on farms has dropped from 90 percent in 1810 to between 2 and 3 percent today; the importance of agriculture, and the attendant government involvement in it, has not diminished.

While on diplomatic missions abroad, Thomas Jefferson and Benjamin Franklin collected rice, olives, and other plants to test on American farms. Crop diversification was important to the new nation with its variety of soils and climates. The first Federal agricultural appropriation in 1839 enabled the Patent Office to collect and distribute foreign seeds. The Office of Foreign Seed and Plant Introduction, established in 1901, sent agricultural explorers to the far reaches of the earth to collect plant materials.

To encourage farmers to test some of these new plants, the U.S. Department of Agriculture (USDA) distributed seeds from 1850 to 1924. The seed packets distributed, up to 1.1 billion at the program's height, were popular with farmers not only because seeds were free, but because government seeds were top quality. In addition to supplying seeds, the USDA tested and taught farming techniques at experiment stations across the country. Hybrid corn is just one of its many experiment station innovations.

Crop and market controls like the Agricultural Adjustment Act (1933), have an impact on our food supply. Since then, government has continued to influence supply and demand through farm subsidies, loans, and price controls.

Farm Family Picnic, undated
Many urbanites held on to the agrarian myth—the belief that the family farm stood for all that is pure and good in America—but demanded the inexpensive food that large agribusiness could supply.

National Archives, Records of the United States Information Agency

FOREIGN PLANT EXPLORATION

Braving scorpions, thieves, disease, and harsh climates, American explorers scoured the earth.

Their quest: giant cabbages, one-pound peaches, and wilt-resistant spinach. Since its inception, the U.S. Government has sought to diversify the nation's food sources with foreign plants. Thomas Jefferson said, "The greatest service which can be rendered any country is to add a useful plant to its culture." This statement was clearly heartfelt; he once risked capital punishment smuggling rice out of Italy in his coat pockets.

Following in the footsteps of the Founding Fathers, the Department of Agriculture sent plant hunters to the far reaches of the earth in search of food plants. From the mid 1800s to the 1930s, these adventurers sought specimens that could weather America's diverse climates and survive in its various soils. Threatened by wild animals, robbers, and hostile government officials, the plant explorers covered thousands of miles of uncharted territory to discover countless varieties of plants. From mangoes, Meyer lemons, and mangosteens to persimmons, pomegranates, and pistachios, many of the foods now grown in the United States sprouted from seeds and shoots gathered on those expeditions.

Mashing Boiled Soybeans in Korea, undated
Explorers documented information about plants, soils, climates, and growing techniques. They were also careful to note the ways plants were used in the local culture.

National Archives, Records of the Bureau of Plant Industry, Soils, and Agricultural Engineering

Apricots, ca. 1906
Frank N. Meyer introduced several new varieties of apricots to the United States, along with hundreds of other plants.

National Archives, Records of the Bureau of Plant Industry, Soils, and Agricultural Engineering

P. H. Dorsett, 1925
P. H. Dorsett, a USDA plant explorer who collected soybeans in Japan, Korea, and Manchurian China, prepares specimens on a makeshift table.

National Archives, Records of the Bureau of Plant Industry, Soils, and Agricultural Engineering

FREE SEEDS FOR FARMERS

Government Seeds:
Agricultural Advancement or Congressional Boondoggle?

The Government's first official effort to improve American agriculture was through seed distribution. In 1839, Congress appropriated $1,000 to the Patent Office to distribute seeds to farmers through their congressional representatives. At the time, there was no commercial seed industry to speak of, and free seeds were seen as a way to encourage farmers to test rare plants. Several decades into the program, the bulk of the mailings contained common variety vegetable and flower seeds. In 1897, at the height of the program, the Government distributed 1.1 billion packets of free seeds to farmers.

The Department of Agriculture, however, questioned whether the expensive program furthered American agriculture. Congress fought to hang on to the popular program, but the nascent seed industry protested against it. In 1924, after a long and intense lobbying effort by the American Seed Trade Association, Congress eliminated the USDA seed distribution program.

RADISH.
French Breakfast.

A small, early, distinctly white tipped, bright scarlet, olive shaped root of excellent quality. Very popular, both as a forcing and outdoor sort.

Culture.—Sow in rich well prepared soil in drills 16 to 24 inches apart dropping 2 to 4 seeds to an inch and covering with three-fourths inch of fine mellow soil. Give frequent and thorough cultivation.

U. S. DEPARTMENT OF AGRICULTURE.
- - Congressional Seed Distribution. - -
Please report the result of your trial to this Department.

Seed Packet, 1903–4

National Archives, Records of the Bureau of Plant Industry, Soils, and Agricultural Engineering

View of Packeting Floor, 1905
The seed distribution program became so large that it had its own building in Washington, DC.

National Archives, Records of the Bureau of Plant Industry, Soils, and Agricultural Engineering

TESTING AND TEACHING

"Farming looks mighty easy when your plow is a pencil and you're a thousand miles from the corn field."
—President Dwight D. Eisenhower

Feeding a growing nation requires innovation. The Hatch Act of 1887 was designed to sow the seeds of creativity in every state of the Union. States received Federal land grants to establish agricultural experiment stations—research centers dedicated to finding solutions and improving methods in agriculture and food production.

The Hatch Act also stipulated that the experiment stations share their agricultural discoveries and methods with farmers. Research undertaken or funded by the USDA resulted in improved farming methods and new strains of plants. These discoveries were then shared with farmers and their families. The exhibits, brochures, and radio scripts they created reflected the creativity and humor invested in these efforts. In undertaking both scientific research and education, the Hatch Act affected the types of foods farmers grew and the methods used to cultivate them.

Pig Cafeteria, undated
Knotting the dinner napkin around the neck of this cloven-hoofed diner, a USDA exhibitor completes "the Pig Cafeteria"—one of many exhibits created to educate farmers. This humorous take on the science of hog nutrition aimed to attract farmers' attention.

National Archives, Records of the Office of the Secretary of Agriculture

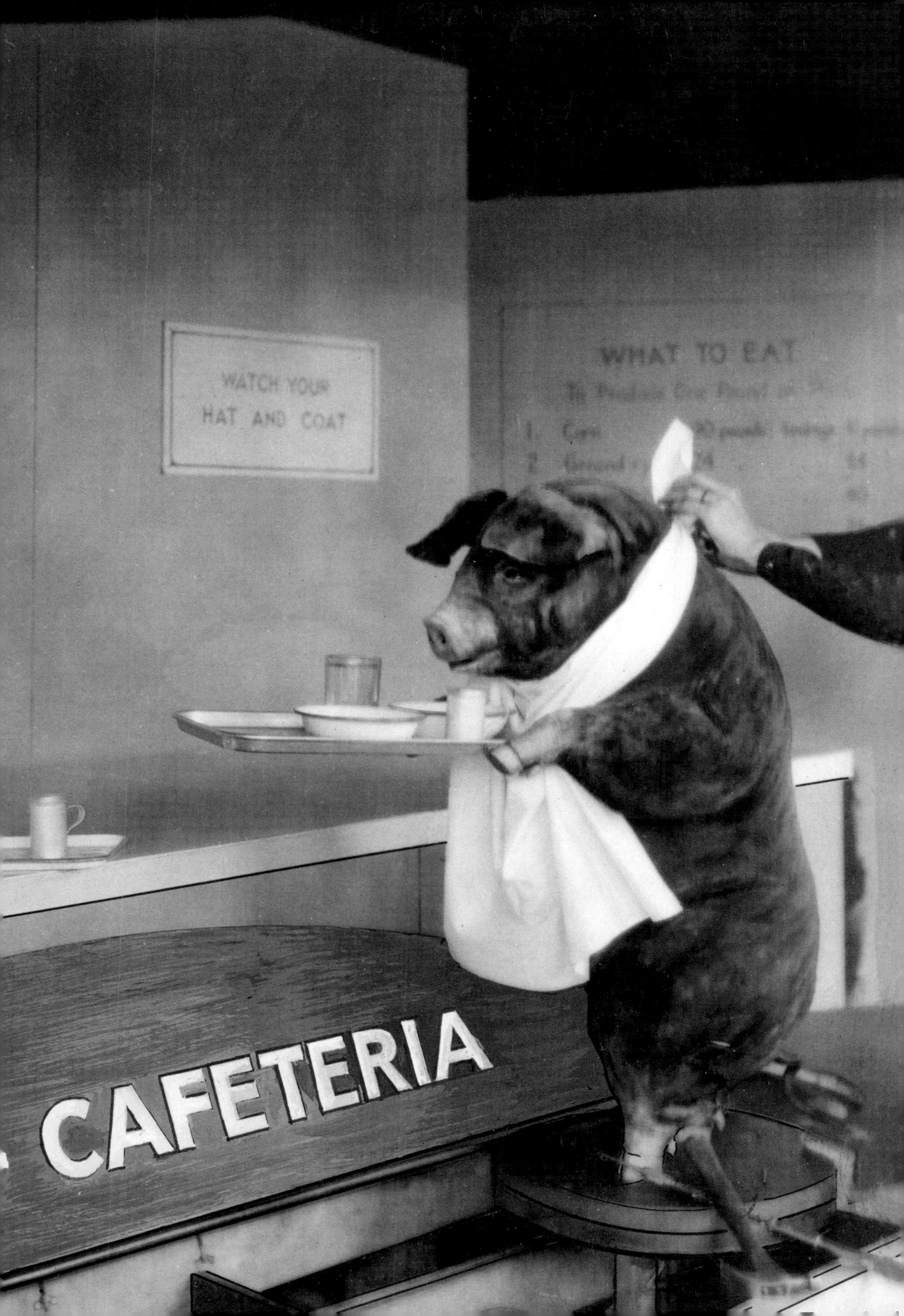
WATCH YOUR
HAT AND COAT
WHAT TO EAT
CAFETERIA

APPLE AND FRUIT EXHIBIT, DEPARTMENT OF AGRICULTURE, GROUP VIII.
~ Paris - France - 1900. ~

Paris Exposition, 1900
The USDA showcased the fruits of its research in expositions across the country and around the world. This apple exhibit was proudly displayed at the Paris Exposition.

National Archives, Records of the Office of the Secretary of Agriculture

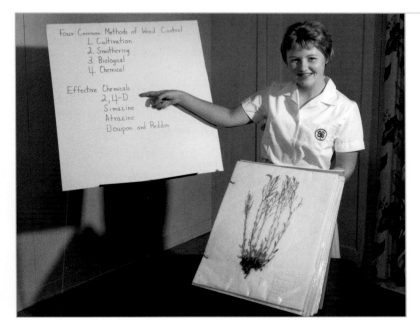

4-H Project, undated
16-year-old Freda Kay Harris chose the subject of weeds and weed control for her 4-H demonstration. Farmers were not always receptive to new ideas, but often their children were willing to experiment. USDA programs like 4-H taught new methods to the kids, who shared their experiences and successes with their parents.

National Archives, Records of the Extension Service

CROP AND MARKET CONTROLS

In times of crisis, perceived and real, farmers looked to the Government to protect their livelihoods. In times of war, the Government enlisted farms in the fight.

In the late 1800s, dairy farmers petitioned the Government to prevent the "oily imposter," margarine, from destroying their livelihoods. Although margarine was perceived to be a threat, the Great Depression was a true agricultural crisis. Reduced demand for farm commodities sent prices spiraling downward. President Franklin D. Roosevelt responded with the 1933 Agricultural Adjustment Act (AAA). The AAA's system of price supports and subsidies remains the basis of America's farm policy—a policy that continues to influence the quality, quantity, price, and variety of foods grown in America.

The other side of the pendulum—inflation—also spurred the Government to action. Eager to prevent prices from skyrocketing during World War II, the Government instituted price control measures and encouraged farmers to grow key crops. Food price inflation in the 1970s inspired protests and boycotts.

The first farm subsidies and land retirement programs were initiated when over 20 percent of the population worked on farms—compared to 2 percent today. American farm policy played a role in the transformation of agriculture from small, labor-intensive family farms to enormous, highly mechanized agribusinesses.

Price Comparison, 1945
These stylish ladies demonstrate what $1.34 bought in 1918 and 1945, thanks to price controls.

National Archives, Records of the Office of Price Administration

1918
bs. Sugar..$1.34

1945
O.P.A. CEILING PRICES:

5 lbs. Sugar	.32
Bread	.09
6 Oranges	.22
2 quarts Milk	.29
Oatmeal	.12
Coffee	.27
	1.3
tax	.0
	$ 1.3

CRIMES AGAINST BUTTER

The prize offered by Emperor Louis Napoleon III for the invention of a butter substitute was claimed by a Frenchman in 1870. American dairy farmers quickly demanded protection from imitation butter. Congress responded with the Margarine Act of 1886—raising margarine's price through taxes and licensing. Amendments to the Margarine Act taxed colored margarine at an even higher rate. Public outcry against margarine taxes mounted as the supply of butter dwindled during and after World War II. Federal margarine taxes were finally repealed in 1950.

Leavenworth Inmate, ca. 1886
John McMonigle ate prison food for almost a year for peddling margarine without a license.

National Archives, Records of the Bureau of Prisons

Mug Shots, 1915
Charles Wille was sent to Leavenworth Federal Penitentiary for trafficking in the "Poor Man's Butter."

National Archives, Records of the Bureau of Prisons

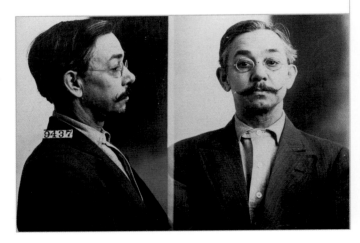

FARM

Bertillon Measurement Card for John Seymour, 1916

Taxes on colored margarine created a boon for bootleggers. But while back-alley dealings in yellow oleo may have been profitable, the penalties were severe. Georgia's John Seymour was sentenced to two years in the state penitentiary for his crimes against butter.

National Archives, Records of the Bureau of Prisons

Farmer's Petition, 1886

"Our soils will be depleted and become barren," "the dairy industry is doomed," and Americans will be robbed of "life promoting vitamins . . . without which human infants cannot continue to live" are just some of the prognostications made by dairy farmers in their petitions for market controls on imitation dairy products.

National Archives, Records of the U.S. House of Representatives

THE FIRST FARM POLICY

"An unprecedented condition calls for new means to rescue agriculture."
—President Franklin D. Roosevelt

The Agricultural Adjustment Act (AAA) was one of the first pieces of legislation Franklin D. Roosevelt introduced after his election in 1933. For the first time, Congress took on the responsibility of balancing supply and demand so that farmers could make a profit. To raise prices, the AAA paid farmers subsidies to leave some of their land fallow. Although some farmers didn't like the idea of having the Federal Government tell them how to farm, few could afford to opt out of the Government payments.

Ever-normal Granary, ca. 1933
The practice of storing surplus grain to keep prices stable or "ever-normal" dates to biblical times. In 1938, the AAA began to make loans to farmers, enabling them to stockpile grain until the market rebounded.

National Archives, Records of the Bureau of Agricultural Economics

Newspaper Article from *Des Moines Tribune*, 1933
The captions in this issue document Iowa farmers' views on farm problems, recovery plans, and the administration in the first year of the Agricultural Adjustment Act.

National Archives, Records of the Office of the Secretary of Agriculture

Jasper, Dallas County Farmer Views

Jasper county and Dallas county farmers, a number of whom were met at random by a Tribune reporter this week, commented on farm problems, recovery plans and the administration.

They discussed their attitude toward President Roosevelt, Secretary of Agriculture Henry Wallace, various proposed plans to aid the farmer, the working of the NRA and the farm holiday.

E. M. Gagle, Route 2, Colfax, owner 480 acres—Wallace may be all right, but it looks to me as if the corn-hog program is working the wrong way. The tax cuts down consumption with production. The cheaper we can get the price to the consumer, the more we will sell, and that will take care of over production. A lot of the trouble is in the profits made by the middlemen. The government should watch that. The state administration is all right, I guess. It's pretty hard to tell about Roosevelt yet, but I'll say this—he's trying. It's too early to judge him. I don't know much about gold and currency problems. I haven't followed the 60-cent corn loan proposal, but that's about what we ought to have.

E. M. GAGLE.

L. H. Burton, Route 2, Colfax, manager, 200 acres—I'm not much in favor of the farm strike and I doubt if it has enough support to get anywhere. Roosevelt's all right. The honest dollar is the best thing to solve the currency problem and Roosevelt's going after it in the right way. There's some criticism of Wallace, but I have a lot of faith in him.

L. H. BURTON.

Owen Gray, Route 2, Bussey—I'm not in favor of the farm strike. It can't work unless all hold together and there are too many farm organizations for that. The NRA hasn't been in effect long enough yet to judge it. It has hurt the farmer so far, but it deserves a fair trial. Roosevelt is all right. He's trying to help all classes. I don't know about Wallace. I don't think there's any such thing as over production—it's under consumption. We shouldn't reduce our crops while there are people who are starving.

OWEN GRAY.

R. W. Williams, Route 2, Colfax, owner, 80 acres—The NRA just started at the wrong end. Sixty per cent of the consumption in the United States is on the farms, so that's where the effort to build buying power should start. I think Roosevelt's all right, though. He's trying, but he's found he's not so familiar with farm problems as he thought. I don't think much of Wallace. This corn-hog production will work a hardship on someone. Of course, I'll take part and cut my acreage if it will help. I haven't followed the monetary policies of the administration closely. Iowa's state officers are all right, I guess.

R. W. WILLIAMS.

E. F. Meckley, Route 1, Colfax, owner 582 acres—Roosevelt has done all he can do to help the farmer and I haven't much fault to find in Wallace. He had to do what Roosevelt wanted when he took office and both he and the president have changed some of their views in the last few months. They'll co-operate, though, and that's important. I don't think much of farm strikes. Why wouldn't I be in favor of the corn-hog program—it means money for me? I don't think it was the thing to do, though. We may be sorry later on for this crop reduction if the weather should take a hand some year. I'm in favor of inflation and think they will inflate in some way later. We'd be better off now with inflated currency. I'm in favor of the NRA if everyone gets behind it. It's hurting the farmer some now but should help him later. It will fail unless all support it, though. I think the whole affair will work itself out all right in a few years if they just let things alone.

E. F. MECKLEY.

Walter Crampe, Route 5, Newton, owner, 225 acres—I don't pay any attention to farm strikes—didn't even know there was one on. I'm no striker, never was. Times like these will always adjust themselves. About Roosevelt, Wallace, and the state administration—I'm not one to condemn anyone. I think Wallace took his job at a bad time. I can't say what's going to happen. I don't know about conditions. If we inflated, what would we do after that was over? Would the pains come back?

Home of Walter Crampe, one of the farmers in Jasper county who commented on the farm problem.

Ralph Sparks, Route 5, Newton, renter, 120 acres—I'm not in favor of farm strikes. The more strikes of any kind you have, the worse you make the country. Lots of farmers who agree to strike don't go through with it anyway. Wallace is too slow with his farm plans. He doesn't do us a bit of good. I'm not in favor of Republicans who take Democratic offices. I'm a Republican, A to Z, so I won't comment on Roosevelt or the state administration. We're no better off now than we were. Corn is a little higher, but the farmer has to pay more for the things he buys. I don't think the NRA is helping anyone. We must have speculation. We can fight the moneyed man all we want to, but we can't get along without him. I'm not in favor of inflation or fooling with the currency. I think we'll be back on the gold standard again in a few years.

RALPH SPARKS.

J. G. Sowers, Route 5, Newton—The farm strike is all right. It should help to raise prices if the strikers stick together. I'm not for the NRA because it would be impossible for farmers to work under the codes, but they enforce them in factories and make things the farmer buys higher. I thought Wallace was O. K. at first, but not now. He's not big enough for the job and he isn't working for the little fellow. I don't believe any plan he has suggested will work. Roosevelt is all right. Inflation might be hard on the rich but they've had the best of the depression so far and I think we might try it. It's getting so that there isn't any middle class any more. They're all poor people. To be honest, the farmer doesn't know what to think.

J. G. SOWERS.

This is the residence of Jacob M. Keller, one of the Dallas county farmers interviewed in a Tribune symposium.

Jacob M. Keller, R. R. 1, Waukee, owns 360 acres—I guess the corn-hog program will be all right if they can make it work. I don't think much of this farm strike. It's pretty hard for the government to help improve farm conditions. NRA hasn't helped us any. I believe Roosevelt's trying; it's a pretty hard proposition and he has a job on his hands. I haven't paid any attention to the state administration. I didn't hear the president's talk about money or read about it. It probably would be all right for the government to loan money on corn.

Clark Wilson, Route 5, Newton, renter, 80 acres—To be honest about it, we haven't had any real hard times here. We've managed to get along, pay the rent, and have a little left. I think the big trouble is that many bought too high and now they don't want to let go. The farm strike won't help out. The longer the farmer holds his produce the bigger the surplus will be when he does start to market it. I think the corn-hog program is all right and that a fellow ought to fall in line with those trying to help out. Inflation and Roosevelt's monetary policies are too deep for me. If all the men who have studied the money problems can't decide on the right one, I hardly think I could. I think it would take a lot of changing around to keep the purchasing power of the dollar stable, though.

H. C. Coffman, R. R. 2, Adel, rents 110 acres—If I have to cut down production on hogs 50 per cent, am I forced to take the same price on the remainder as I would have got on the whole? If a double price would be guaranteed on the remainder, nobody would object. The farm strike's a little radical, although sometimes I think a little radical stuff might help things. If the government would set a peg on grain prices it should help the farmer. The president has power to close our banks and I think he'd have it to put a peg on prices. NRA may have hurt the farmer. It's made the prices of what we have to buy go up. The government should be given credit, for it's trying, at least. I believe Roosevelt means well. I was raised a Republican but I sure voted for him. I believe things could be improved as far as the state administration's concerned. I didn't hear the monetary speech nor read of it. Supposing the government would lend 60 cents on 1,000 bushels of corn and the market never reaches that price? If they charge us 8 per cent interest on the loan, we better sell it for 50 cents.

H. C. COFFMAN.

W. R. Fox, R. R. 1, Waukee, owns 640 acres—The corn program may be all right but I don't think much of including hogs. The farm strike's not the way to get at it. Inflation's the only thing I think might improve farm conditions. NRA isn't helping the farmers any; it's intended for eastern cities. Buying power comes out of the land and if you don't give us a profit, we can't buy. The best thing about Roosevelt so far is that he's trying. Of course I'm a Republican but I didn't vote for Hoover any time. The state administration seems to be doing all right. I haven't read enough about the monetary policy to discuss it. Lending 60 cents a bushel on corn to the farmer would be all right; it would mean quite a bit of money would be spent by them.

W. R. FOX.

R. B. Gloid, Route 1, Monroe—I think it's a shame that there are so many people hungry when things are so cheap. The farm strike won't do any good because the surplus is still on hand when it's over. It's already produced. Supply and demand have a lot to do with prices. I'm no Democrat, but I'll say Roosevelt is trying. Inflation might help the man in debt but it would be hard on the man with money.

Marvin Fox, R. R. 1, Waukee, rents 400 acres—If the corn-hog program will help, get behind it; I believe it will help. I'm in favor of what the government's doing now to improve farm conditions; it's going to help. NRA hasn't affected us as far as having men come looking for work but the farmer's purchasing power is just about what it was a year ago while the price of other things has risen. Roosevelt is doing about as much as he can do—remember he had to create the machinery to do with. I can't see but what the state administration is all right. The government's plan to buy gold seems all right to me. A government loan on corn is fair enough; farmers have borrowed so much, though, that many won't care to go any deeper.

MARVIN FOX.

Gordon Carter, R. R. 1, Dallas Center, owns 640 acres — The corn-hog plan shows the government's trying; it might work out all right. I'm not in favor of the farm strike. I don't know what the government should do to improve farm conditions. I think NRA's a good thing; it hasn't affected us yet but I believe it will in time. Roosevelt's done more about recovery than anyone else has. I think we're all in favor of postponing foreclosures. I didn't hear all the president's monetary talk. A loan on corn might help; if it was 60 cents, farmers could take care of their own troubles.

GORDON CARTER.

Ready for market any time are these hogs on the Gordon Carter farm in Dallas county. Carter says he is holding them for a price increase.

Barns and other buildings on the Gordon Carter farm are shown in this picture.

R. H. Mortimer, Dallas Center, owns 200 acres—I believe the corn-hog plan will be all right, myself. I don't believe in that way of doing things (farm strikes). I firmly believe there should be a bottom pegged on corn, hogs, and some commodities like that. There hasn't been a bottom to anything, the last few years. If a fellow knew where it was, he'd have something to work on. NRA wasn't intended to help the farmer; probably it's made it a little tough on them right now, but if it increases buying power of people it puts back to work it will help us finally. I've been for Roosevelt all the time and I'm still behind him and not going to back up. If he fails after four years I might change my mind. The state administration has been criticized some but I don't see where it's done anything to oppose the farm situation. If Roosevelt's monetary policy will stabilize things, it will be all right; it looks to me like it would do so. Corn should be worth 50 cents as security for credit. Whether a loan on it is a good thing as far as the individual is concerned I can't say.

R. H. MORTIMER.

Deciding her husband needed a "lift" with his corn husking, Mrs. C. A. Brown aided him in his Dallas county farm field when this picture was snapped.

C. A. Brown, R. R. 1, Adel, rents 80 acres—The corn-hog program? Why a fellow doesn't have much of an idea any more what things are going to do. I doubt if the farm strike does any good. The government ought to set a price on corn and hogs; it wouldn't have to be so high just so long as a fellow knew what he was going to get. I don't think much of NRA. I'm surprised such a smart fellow as Roosevelt seems to be would think of such a thing. We're paying twice as much in town as we used to for lots of stuff and getting less for our stuff. It looks to me like Roosevelt started things backward in his recovery plans. Wallace hasn't done a bit of good. I haven't paid any attention to the state administration. I don't know about the monetary policy—I think a dollar's a dollar. If the government would put these prices (of corn) up where they should be, halfway decent, I think everyone would come out all right. Lots of fellows start borrowing money and then can't stop.

L. S. Cook, R. R. 1, Dallas Center, rents 120 acres—I think the plan is fine if you can get everyone to sign up on their actual acreage. Trouble is, a lot will try to fudge a little. I wouldn't just be in favor of that farm strike. The time isn't just right; the administration should be given time to work. I don't know if the government could do much more than it is now to improve things. NRA hasn't made much difference with us out here; that is, I haven't noticed much difference. We've paid a little more for some stuff but a lot of this is probably due to better conditions anyway. I'd like to see labor get the money anyway. I think Roosevelt and his plans are fine. Looks to me like they're doing all they could to get the country in better shape. I've been well satisfied with the state administration so far. Roosevelt's speech last Sunday ought to stimulate production of gold. I believe if we could get a little more money in circulation everybody would spend a little more. I don't care so much for the plan to lend money on corn. By the time you've borrowed on anything like that you usually come out in the hole. Better get prices up to a fair level and stay somewhere near there—make a staple market.

L. S. COOK.

Walter Scott, R. R. 1, Dallas Center, rents 120 acres—This corn-hog program doesn't seem like a good plan, to me, we can't tell what another year is going to bring. I don't know but what these farm strikes may be a pretty good thing. I don't believe in violence, but if farmers would keep it all on their farm they might get a better price for their stuff. If the government had pegged corn when it was 50 cents a bushel it might have helped things. It should help the renters, too, I think. NRA has had no effect on farmers, helpfully. I think some of Roosevelt's plans are all right and some not. The state administration has done some good things and some not so good. I don't approve of that deal up north here last spring. (The assault upon Judge Bradley at Le Mars.) Roosevelt's speech didn't hit on agriculture as much as I thought he would. That corn loan would help. I believe Murphy's doing all he can do.

WALTER SCOTT.

W. H. Keister, Dallas Center, owns 235 acres—What are we going to do with all this vacant land the corn-hog program will make? You can't let the ground lay idle and go to weeds. If there is too much pasture land, it will overdo the cattle question. I have no use for this farm strike. They raise hell around the country with these strikes and where does it end—they have to give in; they can't buck the government. The government's got to put up the price of grain and keep it up. If they put corn up to 50 or 60 cents we might get by. I don't believe NRA is helping the farmer; it's putting what we have to buy, up. Roosevelt is all right and he's doing great. I didn't vote at all last time because I'm a Republican but I wouldn't vote for Hoover. I believe Herring and Murphy are doing all right. The president's monetary policy will be all right, I hope. They've got to do something to cause a change. If a man borrows 60 cents on his corn and can't pay it back, what will the government do? Someone's got to pay it.

W. H. KEISTER.

S. D. Hiatt, R. R. 2, Adel, rents 240 acres—All I've got to say about the corn-hog plan is "here's hoping." This farm strike's all the bunk; you can't force this thing. The government can't peg prices and I don't see how it can do much of anything to improve farm conditions. NRA has been a detriment to the farmer; it has raised prices of what he has to buy and hasn't helped what he has to sell. Roosevelt and his recovery plans look just like a muddle; they try this and they try that. The state administration probably is doing all that it can. I don't know much about the monetary policy; it will be all right, I think, as far as I'm concerned. I don't know if that corn loan will work. Who is the government? It's the people. It may help some people, though.

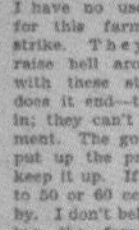

S. D. HIATT.

Location

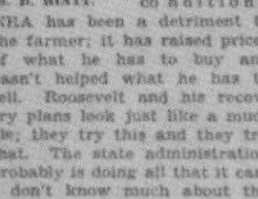

This map shows the location of Jasper and Dallas counties, where farmers discussed the recovery program with a Tribune reporter.

Residence of S. D. Hiatt, in Dallas county. Hiatt is one of a group of farmers interviewed in a Tribune symposium.

E. D. Deemy, R. R. 2, Dallas Center, owns 30 acres—I hardly know what to think of the corn-hog program. I don't know if it will help us much or not. I don't think anything of that farm strike. Pegging prices might be a good stunt to improve farm conditions. I don't think NRA has helped the farmer any; it may have helped the factory man or any of those people. Probably Roosevelt's doing the best he can; he has a big job. Some of 'em say if any other man but Hoover'd been in there we wouldn't be in this shape but I don't agree with that. I never thought very much about the state administration. I hardly know how the monetary policy will work out. It might help some if the government would lend on corn but then what would the government do with it in case the loan wasn't paid back?

E. D. DEEMY.

W. H. Chance, R. R. 1, Adel, owns 115 acres—I've got the same ideas on these things as Skinner has. There wouldn't be any use in my repeating 'em to you.

W. H. CHANCE.

J. L. Brown, R. R. 1, Adel, owns 20 acres—I don't understand that corn-hog plan. It may be all right; I hope it is, but I'm kind of afraid it isn't. I don't believe these farm strikers will get anywhere. I was in hopes it would do some good but I don't believe it will be strong enough. The government should inflate the currency to improve farm conditions. I believe it's our only remedy. So far, NRA has been a bad thing, a detriment, for farmers. Prices of things we had to buy went up. I don't believe Wallace has done anything for us yet. I don't understand the president's plans. He's going to do something for us but it's going to take a long time. He has a hard row to hoe and he hasn't been in long enough to have done much yet. The state administration is trying to do all they can; they can't do much. Taxes are too high yet. I've read something of the monetary policy but I'm not posted on it. Who's going to pay for this corn loan? There's such a thing as spending more than you've got. I don't believe the government should lend it.

J. L. BROWN.

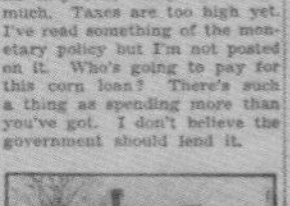

Another Dallas county farm residence—that of J. L. Brown—is shown in this photograph.

R. M. Howard, R. R. 2, Dallas Center, rents 300 acres—The corn-hog plan is all right if they carry it out. I don't think very much of the farm strike; I expect some of them are getting desperate, though. I think this corn-hog proposition will help the farmer as much as anything if they get it going. I don't think NRA has helped the farmer. It may do so later. They've raised the prices of things we have to buy. Husking gloves, for instance, are almost as much as they were during the war. I think Roosevelt's plans are all right. I'm a Republican, but of course I voted for Roosevelt. He's doing all he can but must have co-operation. The state administration is doing a pretty good job. I think the monetary policy is okay; anything that would help, I'm for. That loan idea is all right. The government will be buying a lot of corn. If corn goes to 60 cents the farmer can get along fine.

R. M. HOWARD.

G. R. Royer, Dallas Center, rents 160 acres—If you can get 'em all to do it I believe this corn-hog program will be all right. It don't do any good for part to strike and part not to. That loan on corn would help improve conditions a lot. I can't see that NRA has done any good. More harm than good, for it's brought up the price of everything the farmer has to buy. I believe Roosevelt's plans are all right; he's trying to do something anyway. I'm not much posted on the state administration; I believe Herring's all right. The monetary policy should be all right. I believe that corn loan's the quickest way to get the money out. It will keep the corn off the market and bring the price up.

G. R. ROYER.

Emerson Morgan, Route 4, Newton, renter, 120 acres—I don't think the farm strike will get anywhere without everyone back of it. It will be like coal strikes around here. They'll get little out of it. If they had a 100 per cent layoff for 10 days it would bring prices up, but they'll never have nearly 100 per cent. Wallace means all right, but he has no control over the man not signing crop reduction, so I think Wallace's plans will fall through. I think the money is all right now and they should leave it alone, but set commodity prices. I didn't vote for Roosevelt, but I don't kick as long as he tries to do something. The NRA will knock the little fellow out. Do away with NRA, fix prices to give cost of production, and we'll be all right.

EMERSON MORGAN.

Orville Royer farm home in Dallas county is shown in this picture. Dwyer is one of the farmers questioned in a Tribune symposium.

Orville Royer, R. R. 2, Dallas Center, owns 280 acres—About this corn-hog plan, the fellow who pays for it finally turns out to be the farmer. I don't think it pays to strike. Minimum prices for corn and hogs might help things. If we got more for our crops, we'd hire more help and could pay 'em more. NRA doesn't appear to have had any effect yet except gasoline, flour, and a few other things have gone up a little. I don't approve of destroying crops such as cotton and others. Once they're here, they should be harvested. I don't know so much about the state administration and nothing about the monetary policy. It might be all right to lend 60 cents on corn, if it didn't get any higher than that price. If we'd get 60 cents a bushel for this year's crop, we wouldn't lose much.

A. Crum, Route 2, Monroe, owner, 120 acres—I'm not for farm strikes. The cure should start from the bottom, not after reaching the marketing stage. I'm not for Wallace. A man can't let his ground lie idle after he's built it up, although I know there's some that shouldn't be in production. The NRA won't work. How can a man put others to work with no money to hire them? Roosevelt is doing all he can, but he can't do it all alone. I think inflation or the managed dollar would help some.

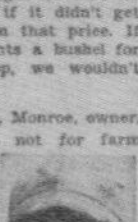

A. CRUM.

W. B. Langmaid, Route 5, Newton, owner, 400 acres—I think somebody else in office would make just as many mistakes as Wallace has, and I think Roosevelt is a dandy fellow. He's broad minded, tries hard, and you can't beat him. I don't know about inflation. I think we should keep the money in proportion to products and that we could avoid hard times that way. Roosevelt's managed dollar plan is good and I think it will work. I haven't followed the plan to lend 60 cents on corn. I'm not in favor of the farm strike.

Here is the residence of W. B. Langmaid, Jasper county farmer who discussed the recovery program with a Tribune reporter.

J. L. Skinner, R. R. 1, Adel, rents 134 acres—I think this corn-hog program is a bad thing. It seems like a shame to kill off hogs when people are starving. The farm strike is the only thing that will get us anywhere. The best thing the government could do to help is to lend money to the farmer at a reasonable rate of interest—4 per cent or 5 per cent. NRA has helped the big cities and made it harder on the farmers. Everything he has to buy went up—nothing he had to sell did. If they'd started with agriculture first we could have paid our hired help more and hired more men. Roosevelt's doing all he possibly can; none of the rest of 'em tried. The state's doing about all it can do. Taxes wouldn't be so much out of line if we got the right price for what we raised. The monetary policy probably will be all right. It would be fine for the government to make that loan on corn. Corn would be a lot better security than those foreign bonds the banks bought.

J. L. SKINNER.

Thomas Webb, Adel, hired man—I don't know what to think of this corn-hog program. There's nothing to this farm strike but I don't know whether it will gain much. The government ought to raise the price of the stuff the farmer has to sell. NRA may help the farmer in time. Roosevelt's doing as good as he can under the circumstances. I believe he's starting too many things and not finishing enough of them. I don't know enough about the state administration to say anything. The same about the speech. That loan on corn would be all right; if the price didn't go up, the government would hold the sack—the farmer's been holding it long enough.

THOMAS WEBB.

Roy Hamblin, Waukee, hired man—I believe the corn-hog program will work all right in time; it's a big problem. I don't believe farm strikes are the right idea; they can't get any place with that kind of stuff. The government's doing about the best it can to improve farm conditions. I think NRA will be okay in time to come. Roosevelt has a real man's job. He's doing as well as or better than anyone we've had in the job for years, but he needs co-operation. I haven't studied much about the state administration but I believe it's doing the best it can. The corn loan should be a good thing to help out.

ROY HAMBLIN.

Oakley Wood, Route 1, Monroe, renter, 240 acres—I haven't followed the farm strike and haven't thought much about Wallace. I've been too busy. Roosevelt is all right, though.

I haven't followed the administration's monetary policies closely enough to say anything about them.

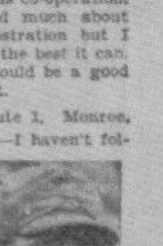

OAKLEY WOOD.

Charles W. Morgan, Route 2, Colfax—The NRA is all right, but it's not helping me any. Roosevelt's all right, too. I'm not in favor of farm strikes. They don't do any good and just get people down on the farmers. Wallace is trying to help out. I think cutting down of production will help the farmer some.

FOOD WILL WIN THE WAR

With the world at war in the 1940s, the Agricultural Adjustment Administration mandate was reversed. "Production!" became the rallying cry. Farmers had to feed the troops, civilians, and overseas allies. They were prodded to grow more corn, soybeans, and sugar beets. The increased demand for food was expected to cause inflation. The Office of Price Administration was established to place ceilings on prices and to ration items that became scarce.

Soybeans Poster, 1944
In wartime, soybeans became important in both North America and Europe as substitutes for other protein foods and as a source of edible oil. This poster from World War II exhorts farmers to grow more soybeans.

National Archives, Records of the Office of the Secretary of Agriculture

Sugar Beets Poster, 1945
Demand for sugar was high during World War II. It was used both for explosives (to create industrial alcohol) and for beverage alcohol. Posters like this one encouraged farmers to convert their fields to sugar beets.

National Archives, Records of the Office of the Secretary of Agriculture

Get Your Farm in the Fight, 1942

National Archives, Records of the Office of the Secretary of Agriculture

FACTORY

The Industrial Revolution transformed life for many 19th-century Americans. Factories brought jobs, urban living, and a new relationship with food. City-dwellers became increasingly removed from the source of their food, leaving them more vulnerable to mishandled and adulterated products. Refrigerated railcars increased the distance food traveled and introduced more opportunities for food to be contaminated or doctored with chemicals. The growing array of convenience foods like ketchup and canned meats also introduced dangers into the household.

Investigators from the Bureau of Chemistry—predecessor to the Food and Drug Administration—examined foods that endangered the health and lives of Americans in the mid to late 1800s. Records from that period reveal tragedies, horrors, and the consequent public outcry for Federal regulation to protect people from dangerous and deceptive additives in foods.

By passing the Pure Food and Drugs Act and Meat Inspection Act in 1906, the Government had accepted a new role: protecting consumers. Regulators for the new Food and Drug Administration were on a mission to protect American consumers from spoiled, rotten, poisoned, and adulterated foods.

Records in the National Archives tell compelling stories about the food revolution that coincided with the Industrial Revolution, the calls for and against government regulation of the food industry, and the increasingly technological methods of food processing.

Candy Factory Inspection, ca. 1908
Before the Pure Food and Drugs Act, factory conditions were horrific. This candy factory was probably scrubbed for inspection.

National Archives, Records of the Food and Drug Administration

FOOD FRIGHTS

An age of suspiciously green peas, deadly candy, and perfumed meat.

Copper sulphate, boric acid, formaldehyde, coal tar, saltpeter . . . sound appetizing? You might have ingested these substances if you had purchased food in America a century ago. And, unless you were a chemist, you might not have known it. Not only were these additives commonly used to preserve foods or disguise foods already spoiled, but food labels rarely reported more than the name and manufacturer of the product. Without a regulating body, the industry was free to use any substance it chose to color, disguise, or prolong the freshness of products. Buying food for the family was a dangerous and sometimes even deadly enterprise.

Our Mutual Friend, 1885
This cartoon published on the cover of the popular magazine *Puck* shows that the use of dangerous additives in candy was widespread. Pictured are a doctor and a sexton (the caretaker of a church and its graveyard) greeting their "mutual friend," a stick of candy.

Courtesy of the FDA History Office

Food Adulteration Notebook, ca. 1890
In this tiny notebook, an investigator wrote, "This sample of candy requires a very careful examination. After eating of it—one child died and two others were taken sick."

National Archives, Records of the Bureau of Agricultural and Industrial Chemistry

I Purchased of Schuster
& Knox, Schuyler, Nebr.

Samples

No. 1 - Colored Candy.
       Manufactured by
       Bunte & Frank, Chicago
Note. This sample of
Candy requires a very
careful examination.
After eating of it — one
1 ℔ 15 c child died, and two
       others were taken sick.
June 13 Altho' it has not yet
       been shown that the said
       bad effects proceeded
       from the Candy, it is
       very strongly suspicious.

       No. 2 - Candy. Manuf. by
       Peycke Candy Co.
12 ½   Omaha, Nebr.
Jn 13

THE POISON SQUAD

Twelve men volunteer to eat meals containing increasing amounts of potentially harmful substances. Sound like reality TV? In fact, it was a USDA Bureau of Chemistry experiment initiated in 1902 to provide support for a national food and drug policy. Chief Chemist Harvey W. Wiley wanted to prove that common chemical preservatives—like borax, sulfuric acid, and formaldehyde—were harmful. He decided to test them—on humans. The experiment surprised Wiley on two counts: the fascination it held for the press, who gleefully dubbed it "The Poison Squad," and the severity of the illness caused by the adulterants. News of the Poison Squad contributed to the mounting public outcry for protection.

Wiley's Notes, 1906
Wiley recorded his subjects' headaches, nausea, and vomiting in his meticulous notes. Although there was no official follow-up, anecdotal reports suggest that none of the volunteers suffered any long-term harm.

National Archives, Records of the Food and Drug Administration

Wiley in Lab, 1906
Dr. Harvey W. Wiley (wearing suit) was the first commissioner of the Food and Drug Administration.

Courtesy of the Washingtoniana Division, DC Public Library

TAINTED MEAT

The sausage-eating public demanded reform after reading about horrific conditions in the meatpacking industry in Upton Sinclair's 1906 novel, *The Jungle*. Although President Theodore Roosevelt considered the author a "crackpot," he had reason to believe Sinclair's allegations. During the Spanish-American War, Roosevelt saw hundreds of soldiers become ill—some fatally—after eating canned meats. Roosevelt responded to Sinclair promising, "the specific evils you point out shall, if their existence be proved, and if I have power, be eradicated."

Postcard Circulated in South Africa Ridiculing the Chicago Meatpacking Industry, 1907

National Archives, General Records of the Department of State

Letter from Upton Sinclair to President Roosevelt, 1907
Upton Sinclair had hoped his book would inspire labor reform. His disappointment that the public focused on the meatpacking industry instead is reflected in his famous statement, "I aimed at the public's heart, and by accident I hit it in the stomach."

National Archives, Records of the Office of the Secretary of Agriculture

The Jungle Publishing Co.

Publishers of the books of Upton Sinclair.

P. O. Box 2064, New York City.

(Letters intended for Upton Sinclair personally should be addressed to Princeton, N. J.)

"The Jungle," a Story of Packingtown.

The "Uncle Tom's Cabin" of wage slavery.—JACK LONDON.

The greatest novel written in America in fifty years.
—DAVID GRAHAM PHILLIPS

King Midas: A Romance.
The Journal of Arthur Stirling.
Prince Hagen: A Phantasy.
Manassas: A Novel of the War.

March 10, 1906.

President Theodore Roosevelt,
Washington, D. C.

My dear President Roosevelt:

I have just returned from some exploring in the Jersey glass factories and find your kind note. I am glad to learn that the Department of Agriculture has taken up the matter of inspection, or lack of it, but I am exceedingly dubious as to what they will discover. I have seen so many people go out there and be put off with smooth pretences. A man has to be something of a detective, or else intimate with the workingmen, as I was, before he can really see what is going on. And it is becoming a great deal more difficult since the publication of "The Jungle." I have received to-day a letter from an employe of Armour & Company, in response to my request to him to take Ray Stannard Baker in hand and show him what he showed me a year and a half ago. He says: "He will have to be well disguised, for 'the lid is on' in Packingtown; he will find two detectives in places where before there was only one." You must understand that the thing which I have called the "condemned meat industry," is a matter of hundreds of thousands of dollars a month. I see in to-day's "Saturday Evening Post" that Mr. Armour declares in his article (which I happen to know is written by George Horace Lorimer) that "In Armour and Company's business not one atom of any

Uncle Sam begins to help buyers beware.

The long-held opposition to Federal food and drug regulation finally crumbled under combined public and political pressure. Even the large packing houses and food processors eventually supported the legislation—especially when the Government agreed to pay for the inspections. They realized that a government seal of approval could restore consumer confidence in their products. President Theodore Roosevelt signed both the Pure Food and Drugs Act and the Meat Inspection Act on June 30, 1906. Afterward, the Federal Government found itself in the business of protecting Americans from unsafe steak, misbranded mushrooms, and tainted tomatoes.

Labels Submitted for Patent, 1882–1906
As soon as the Pure Food and Drugs Act was passed, product labels began to proclaim the purity of their ingredients. But what were those ingredients? It wasn't until 1965 that manufacturers were required to list them.

National Archives, Records of the Patent and Trademark Office

Inspection of Bananas in Baltimore, Maryland, ca. 1906

National Archives, Records of the Food and Drug Administration

The Pure Food and Drugs Act, 1906

The Pure Food and Drugs Act made it illegal to ship or receive any adulterated or misbranded food or drug. To remove foods deemed "filthy, decomposed, or putrid" from the market, FDA agents had to build scientific and legal cases against them.

Egg Seizure, ca. 1908
FDA inspectors seize crates of contaminated eggs.

National Archives, Records of the Food and Drug Administration

Contaminated Ketchup, 1909
Before the Pure Food and Drugs Act, most ketchup was made from fermented tomato cores and skins and dyes to make it red. Because the resulting concoction was prone to explode, benzoate of soda was added as a preservative. Henry Heinz proved ketchup could be made without benzoate in a clean factory using ripe tomatoes.

National Archives, Records of the Food and Drug Administration

Made from Decomposed Material.   Prosecuted
July 3, 1909.   Fined $50.   N. J. 388.

THE MEAT INSPECTION ACT, 1906

The Meat Inspection Act, unlike the Pure Food and Drugs Act, provided for inspection and approval before products went to market. The newly scrubbed meatpacking houses were well-documented by inspectors.

Cudahy Sausage Department, 1910
"The sausage girls were moved upstairs where they could get sun and light."
—From a report on packinghouse reforms after *The Jungle* was published.

National Archives, Records of the Bureau of Animal Industry

Meat Inspection, ca. 1906

National Archives, Records of the Food and Drug Administration

Standard Pekoe and Regulation Oolong

Coffee has overtaken America's original favorite hot beverage—tea. At the time the Tea Inspection Act was passed in 1882, a substantial amount of the tea exported to America was adulterated to increase its weight and to disguise inferiority. Although tea was not the only—or the worst—threat to the health and safety of consumers, it was the easiest to control. Congress already had the power to regulate imports, the source of most of the tea brewed in America.

Tea Tasting, 1931
The National Board of Tea Experts established by the Tea Act of 1897 met annually to set standards for imported tea from 1897 until the act was repealed in 1996.

National Archives, Records of the Food and Drug Administration

Tea Inspection Act, 1882
This act to "prevent the importation of adulterated and spurious teas" was passed in 1882. It was replaced in 1897 with a more comprehensive act that gave the Secretary of the Treasury the authority to adopt Federal tea standards.

National Archives, General Records of the United States Government

Forty-seventh

Congress of the United States, At the second Session,

Begun and held at the CITY OF WASHINGTON, in the DISTRICT OF COLUMBIA, on Monday, the *fourth* day of December, eighteen hundred and eighty-*two*

AN ACT

To prevent the importation of adulterated and spurious Teas.

Be it enacted *by the Senate and House of Representatives of the United States of America in Congress assembled,* That from and after the passage of this act, it shall be unlawful for any person or persons or corporation to import or bring into the United States any merchandise for sale as tea, adulterated with spurious leaf or with exhausted leaves, or which contains so great an admixture of chemicals or other deleterious substances as to make it unfit for use; and the importation of all such merchandise is hereby prohibited.

Sec. 2. That on making entry at the custom house of all tea or merchandise described as tea imported into the United States, the importer or consignee shall give a bond to the collector of the port that such merchandise shall not be removed from warehouse until released by the custom house authorities, who shall examine it with reference to its purity and fitness for consumption; and that for the purpose of such examination samples of each line in every invoice shall be submitted by the importer or consignee to the examiner, with his written statement that such samples represent the true quality of each and every part of the invoice, and accord with the specification therein contained; and in case the examiner has reason to believe that such samples do not represent the true quality of the invoice, he shall make such further examination of the tea represented by the invoice, or any part thereof, as shall be necessary; Provided, That such further examination of such tea shall be made within three days after entry thereof has been made at the custom-house; And provided further, That the bond above required shall also be conditioned for the payment of all custom house charges which may attach to such merchandise prior to its being released or

KITCHEN

Eat more protein and fewer carbohydrates. These familiar recommendations came from Wilbur Olin Atwater in the 1890s. Atwater conducted the first federally funded nutrition research in the United States. His seminal studies contributed to the growing awareness of the varying amount of energy in foods. Prior to Atwater, most Americans considered food to be food. It didn't matter what you ate, only how much.

When Atwater's findings were translated for consumers in 1916, the food guide was born. The USDA hired practitioners of the fledgling field of home economics to write these guides and lead nutrition programs through the Cooperative Extension Service. Eschewing the "pinch of this, dab of that" tradition, home economists' scientific approach to cooking made it easier to quantify the nutritional values of their recipes.

During World Wars I and II, nutrition became not just a matter of public health, but of national security. To provide adequate nutrients for soldiers and civilians, the Government ramped up its nutrition education programs. With certain foods in scarce supply, the understanding of food substitutes, like beans for meat, was critical.

In his crusade to improve the nutritional quality of meals produced in American kitchens, Uncle Sam has funded groundbreaking research, deployed an army of home economists into the kitchens and classrooms of America, and plastered public spaces with pie charts and pyramids. Pitted against cultural traditions, advertising, and socioeconomic forces, the quest to change American eating habits has been an uphill battle.

Woman Weighing Broccoli, undated
Demonstrating the serious scientific approach to home economics, this nutritionist weighs broccoli for a study.

National Archives, Records of the Bureau of Human Nutrition and Home Economics

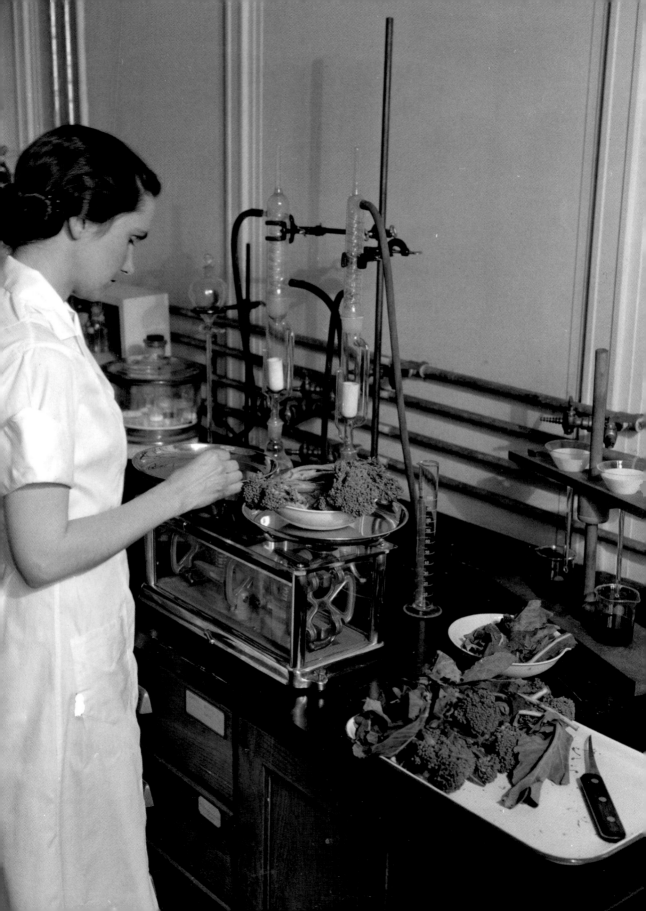

NUTRITION: BREAKING IT DOWN

"The evils of overeating may not be felt at once, but sooner or later they are sure to appear—perhaps in an excessive amount of fatty tissue, perhaps in general debility, perhaps in actual disease."
—W. O. Atwater

Fat, protein, carbohydrates, calories—thanks to W. O. Atwater, these words entered the consciousness of Americans in the 1890s. As Special Agent in Charge of Nutrition Investigations in the Office of Experiment Stations, Atwater was one of the first Americans to undertake scientific human nutrition studies. He quantified the energy values (calories) of different types of food. By establishing the amount of energy expended in different activities, he was able to calculate the number of calories required to maintain a healthy body. His discoveries formed the basis of today's knowledge of nutrition.

Subject in Calorimeter, undated
Atwater and his team used a respiration calorimeter to measure the heat produced and the metabolic rate of individuals performing different activities. Inside the chamber, volunteers read, ironed, and rode stationary bicycles. This cutting-edge technology cost over $10,000 annually to operate in the 1890s.

National Archives, Records of the Bureau of Human Nutrition and Home Economics

Respiration Calorimeter, ca. 1899

National Archives, Records of the Bureau of Human Nutrition and Home Economics

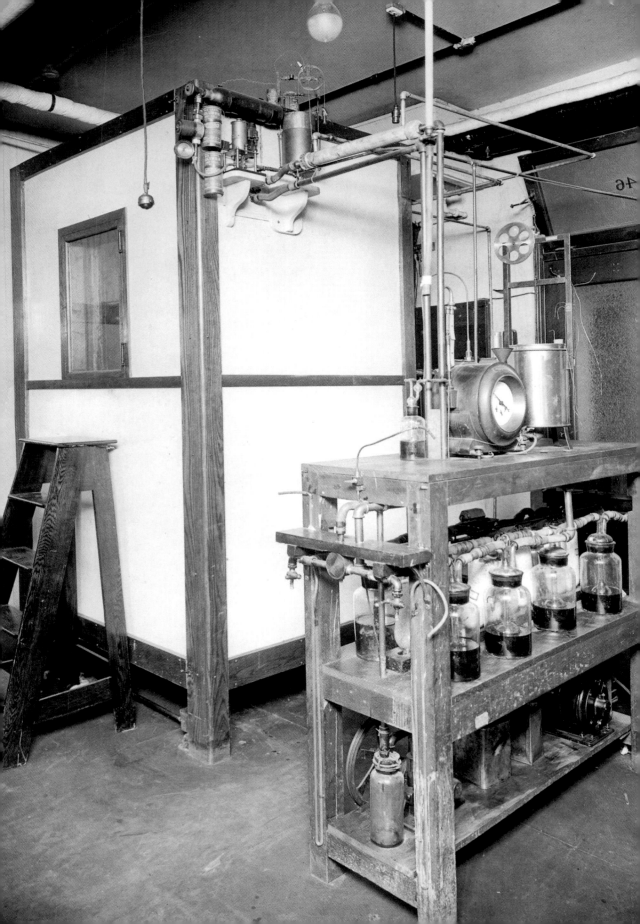

EAT IT—BECAUSE IT'S GOOD FOR YOU!

The American public's growing awareness of the science of nutrition came at a price: "because it tastes good" was no longer considered a sound basis for food choices.

Ever since the first food guide was published in 1894, Uncle Sam has tried to persuade Americans to eat nutritious foods. But "what's good for us" is a moving target. The number of food groups, for example, topped out at 12 in the 1930s, went down to 7 during World War II, and was cut back to 4 in 1956, before 5 food groups were assembled into the Food Guide Pyramid in 1992. Vitamins were unknown when the first nutrition studies were done in America, so fruits and vegetables played a minor role in the food guides of the early 1900s. Malnutrition became a concern in the 1930s—the emphasis then was on getting enough nutrients. In the 1970s, food guides began to warn against over-consumption of certain foods, like those high in cholesterol. Now that obesity has become a major problem, Uncle Sam is urging Americans to eat in moderation and pursue an active lifestyle.

Signs of Good Nutrition Poster, 1931
How was a mother to know if her child was truly well-nourished? She could look for the "signs of good nutrition" illustrated in this poster. After child labor was abolished and compulsory education laws established, child welfare advocates turned their attention to the care and feeding of children.

National Archives, Records of the Office of Education

Signs of Good Nutrition

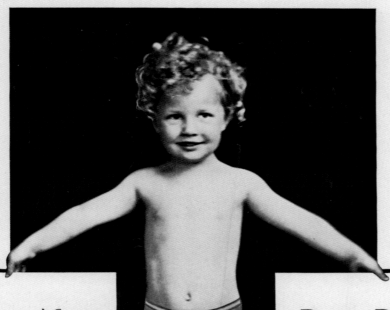

Happy, Alert Expression

Sound Even Teeth

Deep, Broad Chest

Strong Straight Legs

A Sturdy Body and Regular Gain in Height and Weight

CHILD-FEEDING CHART 2

Bureau of Home Economics

UNITED STATES DEPARTMENT OF AGRICULTURE

U. S. GOVERNMENT PRINTING OFFICE: 1931 6—7622

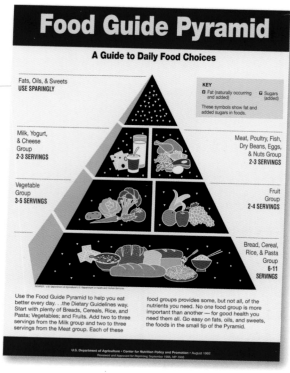

Food Guide Pyramid
A Guide to Daily Food Choices

Food Pyramid Poster, 1992
In 1992, the USDA published its first food pyramid—a graphic illustration designed to convey the principles of a healthy diet in an easy-to-understand visual diagram.

National Archives, Records of the Food and Nutrition Service

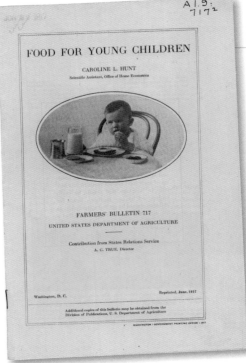

Food for Young Children Pamphlet, 1917
USDA nutritionist Caroline Hunt created this food guide for children. She categorized foods into five groups: milk and meat, cereals, vegetables and fruits, fats and fatty foods, and sugars and sugary foods.

National Archives, Publications of the U.S. Government

Food Group Poster, ca. 1945
Some might like to reinstate this food guide from World War II because butter has its own food group and the food guide recommends eating any other foods desired in addition to the Basic Seven.

National Archives, Records of the Office of Government Reports

For Health...eat some food from each group...every day!

GROUP ONE

GREEN AND YELLOW VEGETABLES...
some raw—some cooked, frozen or canned

GROUP TWO

ORANGES, TOMATOES, GRAPEFRUIT...
or raw cabbage or salad greens

GROUP THREE

POTATOES AND OTHER VEGETABLES AND FRUITS
raw, dried, cooked, frozen or canned

GROUP FOUR

MILK AND MILK PRODUCTS...
fluid, evaporated, dried milk, or cheese

GROUP FIVE

MEAT, POULTRY, FISH, OR EGGS...
or dried beans, peas, nuts, or peanut butter

GROUP SIX

BREAD, FLOUR, AND CEREALS...
Natural whole grain—or enriched or restored

GROUP SEVEN

BUTTER AND FORTIFIED MARGARINE
(with added Vitamin A)

U.S. NEEDS US STRONG
★ EAT THE BASIC 7 EVERY DAY ★

U. S. GOVERNMENT CHART

IN ADDITION TO THE BASIC 7... EAT ANY OTHER FOODS YOU WANT

U.S. DEPARTMENT OF AGRICULTURE

NUTRITION CLAIMS

Scientists made new discoveries about vitamins in the early 1900s. Subsequently, the understanding of the importance of vitamins gradually entered public consciousness. Before the development of practical methods of measuring them, advertisers seized the opportunity to make unsubstantiated claims about the healthful properties of their foods.

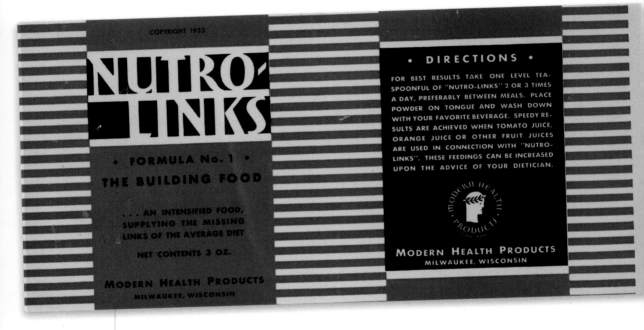

Nutro-Links Intensified Food Label Submitted for Patent, ca. 1930–40
At the time, the Modern Health Products Company was under no obligation to define what "missing links" this "intensified food" supplied.

National Archives, Records of the Patent and Trademark Office

Grains of Health, 1906
This product claims to be "more wholesome and nourishing than any of the Cereal Drinks, Tea, Coffee and Cocoa," but it is unclear what it is, much less what type and amount of nutrients it offers.

National Archives, Records of the Patent and Trademark Office

Grains of Health
A COFFEE
IN TASTE
IN FLAVOR
A DRINK FOR
Morning
Noon
and
Night.
A DRINK FOR THE YOUNG AND THE OLD.
A DRINK FOR THE SICK AND THE WELL.
ALL THE WORLD REACHES FOR IT!
IT REACHES ALL THE WORLD.
A MIXTURE.
Far more Palatable, Wholesome and Nourishing than any of the Cereal Drinks, Tea, Coffee and Cocoa. It is so prepared that the strongest and the most delicate person may drink it at the same table
GRAINS OF HEALTH FOOD COFFEE CO.,
CLEVELAND.
NEW YORK.
CHICAGO.

TRADING APRONS FOR LAB COATS

"Home Economics stands for . . . the utilization of all the resources of modern science to improve home life."
—Ellen Swallow Richards, Founder of the Home Economics Movement, 1904

The Cooperative Extension Service of the USDA, established in 1908, helped elevate the work of putting up preserves and packing lunch pails to a field of study. By providing jobs for home economists and publishing their research, the Government helped this new discipline to become established as a legitimate science. The movement's scientific approach to food and application of business principles to the home changed the way Americans eat.

Hitting their stride in the 1930s, home economists emphasized simple meals with nutritional content that could be easily calculated. Dishes with numerous ingredients, seasonings, and multistep cooking procedures were considered inefficient and nutritionally dubious. They came to see the homemaker's principle job as one of wise consumption rather than skilled production.

Pie Judging Contest, ca. 1920
Dr. Louise Stanley, first head of the Department of Home Economics, judges pies with Mary Lindsay.

National Archives, Records of the Bureau of Human Nutrition and Home Economics

Home Economist Preparing Turkey for Cooking Method Test, undated

National Archives, Records of the Bureau of Human Nutrition and Home Economics

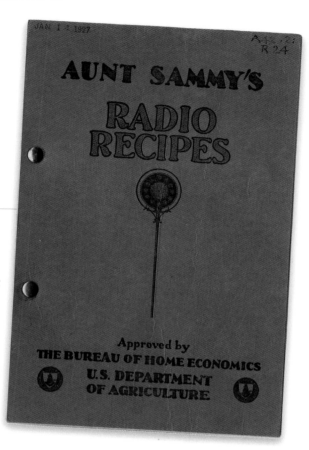

Aunt Sammy's Radio Recipes, 1931
In 1926, the USDA did some
matchmaking for Uncle Sam. They
created a character named "Aunt
Sammy" to teach domestic science over
the radio. So many requests came in
for her recipes—like watermelon pickle
and asparagus on toast—that the
USDA published this booklet in 1931.

*National Archives, Publications of the
U.S. Government*

4-H Demonstration, ca. 1950
Home economists helped
standardize a simple meat,
potato, and vegetable
combination as the typical
American meal. It was easier
to calculate the nutritional
value of simple dishes with
few ingredients. Elaborate,
multi-step cooking methods
didn't meet the efficiency
standards of the home
economist.

*National Archives, Records of
the Extension Service*

EATING FOR UNCLE SAM

To "Keep America Strong," Government ramped up nutrition education efforts during World Wars I and II.

They were outnumbered. The enemy was entrenched. Their resources were limited. But nothing stopped the Government from waging war against the eating habits of the American people. The Government made its most concerted efforts to affect the diets of Americans during World Wars I and II. The battle was fought with squadrons of celebrities, anthropologists, and cartoon characters, as well as a flotilla of films, radio programs, pledge drives, and posters. Often, recent nutrition discoveries provided a nutritional basis for the changes being advocated.

There were some victories. During World War I, the middle and upper classes conserved food by about 15 percent. And in World War II, Americans ate more fresh fruits and vegetables—but largely because canned goods were rationed.

Sugar, Save it Poster, ca. 1917
Sugar was in short supply in both World Wars I and II. Sugar conservation was voluntary during World War I but rationing was necessary during World War II.

National Archives,
Records of the United States
Food Administration

Potatriots, photo detail, ca. 1917–18
This inventive store display promotes the potato as a "good soldier" and recommends people eat it "uniform and all."

National Archives, Records of the United States Food Administration

NATIONAL NUTRITION PROGRAM

In the 1930s, some nutrition scientists believed they had evidence that one-third of Americans were malnourished. As part of the war effort in the 1940s, the Federal Security Agency was tasked with addressing "vitamin starvation." Their solution: "Recommended Daily Allowances," flour enrichment programs, and a government seal to identify nutritious foods. They hired prominent social scientists to apply their insights into culture and human behavior to the campaign to change eating habits. What were the effects of these programs? Small potatoes. Until rationing forced them to change, Americans continued to eat much as they always had.

Wheatena Promotion, 1942
The Nutrition Division of the Federal Security Agency designed a logo for foods with government-approved nutritional value. At first they were flooded with requests for the official endorsement. But food companies soon realized they could tie nutrition claims to the war effort without official government sanction.

National Archives, Records of the Agricultural Marketing Service

Eat Nutritional Food Poster, 1942
The Office of Defense Health and Human Welfare Services produced this poster as part of their World War II nutrition campaign. Eggs were later removed as a separate food group in anticipation of food shortages.

National Archives, Records of the Agricultural Marketing Service

EAT NUTRITIONAL FOOD

Every day, eat this way

MILK & MILK PRODUCTS

...at least a pint for everyone—more for children—or cheese or evaporated or dried milk.

BREAD and CEREAL

...whole grain products or enriched white bread and flour.

ORANGES, TOMATOES, GRAPEFRUIT

...or raw cabbage or salad greens—at least one of these.

MEAT, POULTRY or FISH

...dried beans, peas or nuts occasionally.

GREEN or YELLOW VEGETABLES

...one big helping or more—some raw, some cooked.

EGGS

...at least 3 or 4 a week, cooked any way you choose—or in "made" dishes.

OTHER VEGETABLES, FRUITS

...potatoes, other vegetables or fruits in season.

BUTTER and OTHER SPREADS

...vitamin-rich fats, peanut butter and similar spreads.

Then eat other foods you also like

DO YOUR PART IN THE NATIONAL NUTRITION PROGRAM

Office of Defense Health and Welfare Services. Paul V. McNutt, Director, Washington, D. C.

PATRIOTS EAT DOUGHNUTS

Around 1940, the results of two small studies set off a panic. A handful of subjects deprived of Vitamin B1 (thiamine) became sluggish and apathetic. One researcher concluded that thiamine deficiency was causing Americans to lack energy and motivation—conditions a country mobilizing for war could not afford. Consequently, the Government endorsed products enriched with thiamine. After many letters, the Nutrition Division allowed the Doughnut Corporation to call their product "enriched flour donuts" but not "enriched donuts" or their original choice, "vitamin donuts."

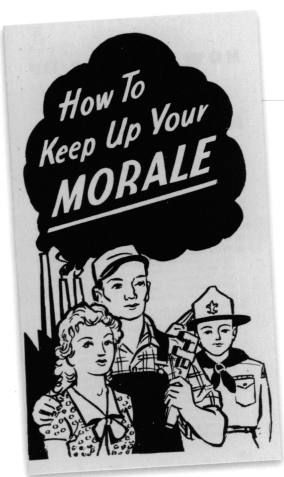

How To Keep Up Your Morale Pamphlet, ca. 1942
This pamphlet accompanied the materials sent by the Doughnut Corporation of America to the Nutrition Division. It explained how eating donuts helped "keep up your morale," the patriotic duty of every American.

National Archives, Records of the Agricultural Marketing Service

Vitamin Donuts Poster, ca. 1942
The National Nutrition Division declined to endorse the term "Vitamin Donuts."

National Archives, Records of the Agricultural Marketing Service

For
PEP *and* **VIGOR—**

VITAMIN

DONUTS

MARK OF
TESTED QUALITY

Each Donut Fortified with a minimum of 25 units of Vitamin B1

POSTER PERSUASION

Posters were at the heart of wartime campaigns to change American eating habits. WWI posters spelled out the reasons why conservation was necessary. They were somber and appealed to a sense of patriotism and virtue. WWII posters used the colorful, upbeat imagery of advertising. They showed Americans that with careful planning, housewives could provide plenty of nutritious food for their families. During both wars, home economists reviewed campaign recommendations to ensure they were nutritionally sound.

Cottage Cheese Poster, ca. 1918
The World War I Food Administration under Herbert Hoover encouraged conservation by promoting "Wheatless Wednesdays" and "Meatless Mondays." This poster suggests cottage cheese as a protein substitute for meat.

National Archives, Records of the United States Food Administration

Eat More Fish Poster, ca. 1918
In the early 1900s, USDA nutrition scientist W. O. Atwater began to make Americans aware that foods could be categorized as proteins, fats, and carbohydrates. The Food Administration helped communicate this message through their campaign to get Americans to substitute fish, beans, and cheese for meat.

National Archives, Records of the United States Food Administration

Save the products of the Land

Eat more fish —
   they feed themselves.

CHARLES LIVINGSTON BULL

UNITED STATES FOOD ADMINISTRATION

Little AMERICANS
Do your bit

Eat Oatmeal-Corn meal mush-
Hominy - other corn cereals -
and Rice with milk.
Save the wheat for our soldiers.

Leave nothing on your plate

UNITED STATES FOOD ADMINISTRATION

NO. 21

Know Your Onions Poster, ca. 1942
Apparently, there was no shortage of onions during World War II.

National Archives, Records of the Office of Government Reports

Home Canning Poster, ca. 1941
Seventy-five percent of Americans rallied to the cause by pickling and preserving fruits and vegetables during World War II. The home canning troops did conserve food, but they weren't without casualties. Cuts, burns, and botulism were some of the calamities suffered by first-time canners.

National Archives, Records of the Office of Government Reports

World War I Garden Poster, ca. 1917
With canned goods in short supply during World Wars
I and II, people ate more fresh fruit and vegetables—
many from their own back yards. It has been estimated
that 40 percent of the fresh produce consumed during
World War II was homegrown.

National Archives, Publications of the U.S. Government

**Groundwork for Victory
Poster, ca. 1944**
The USDA estimates that
more than 20 million victory
gardens were planted during
World War II.

*National Archives, Records of the
Office of Government Reports*

Groundwork for Victory

TEXACO
REG.T.M.

GARDEN
FOR
VICTORY

GROW MORE IN '44

SHORTAGES AND SUSPICION

When rumors of food shortages circulated during World War II, some Americans responded by stampeding grocery stores and hoarding food supplies. Rationing was instituted when voluntary conservation methods proved inadequate. Black markets popped up for meat and other prized items. The Government's attempts to convince cynical members of the public that rationing ensured a fair share for everyone didn't prevent the spread of conspiracy theories. Some cynics believed that the Government fabricated food shortages to keep citizens emotionally invested in the war.

Sixth Graders Learn About War Ration Book Two, 1943
These eager school children are learning about one of the new rationing programs introduced by the Government. In reality, changes in the rationing system caused chaos and confusion for many people.

National Archives, Franklin D. Roosevelt Presidential Library and Museum

Sugar Rationing, ca. 1943
Nutritionists promoted WWII's sugar shortage as an opportunity for Americans to break their sugar habit. Fat chance. People hoarded their weekly half-pound of sugar with surprising fervor.

National Archives, Records of the Office of War Information

TABLE

The most direct way the Government affects what Americans eat is by cooking for them. There are two groups of Americans routinely called to Uncle Sam's table: soldiers and school children. Many eating habits have been altered as a result. Mid-20th-century mess halls and school cafeterias served ethnically diverse populations. For some, especially first-generation Americans, Uncle Sam's cooking was foreign—white bread was a revelation for many children of immigrants. Some came to prefer this "American" food and began to ask for it at home.

In the 1940s, nutritionists standardized menus for the military to ensure troops were ingesting enough vitamins and nutrients. The Armed Forces couldn't afford to have spice-averse soldiers skip meals or spurn "exotic" fruits and vegetables, so regional specialties and ethnic dishes were scrubbed. The National School Lunch Program also operated under strict nutritional guidelines, and, like military food, "Americanized" a generation of taste buds. Federal involvement in school lunch began as an effort to stabilize the price of farm commodities during the Great Depression. The USDA purchased surplus foods and donated them to schools. When President Harry Truman signed the School Lunch Act in 1946, its intent was still to serve agriculture, but also to strengthen children through good nutrition, and thereby, strengthen the nation.

Uncle Sam sets his most elegant and idiosyncratic table for an elite group: the Presidents of the United States and their guests. White House fare usually reflects the personal tastes of its occupants. The individuals who have orchestrated meals for the Presidents include a world-class French chef (John F. Kennedy), a housekeeper (Franklin Roosevelt), and even an army quartermaster (Ulysses S. Grant). Over the years, Americans who wanted to eat in Presidential style—be it high brow or low—have requested their recipes.

Passover Seder Dinner, 1919
The Jewish Welfare Board provided this Passover Seder dinner to Jewish men in the American Expeditionary Forces, Paris, France.

National Archives, Records of Naval Districts and Shore Establishments

158474

SQUARE MEALS FOR SOLDIERS

Although World War II soldiers routinely complained about the "chow," many picked up eating habits in mess halls.

The military is one group that is regularly subjected to Uncle Sam's cooking. Beginning in the 1940s, dieticians standardized military menus—carefully calculating nutritional content and scouring out all but the most familiar and popular dishes. In other words, "heaven sent them meat, but the devil sent them nutritionists." Soldiers from a variety of regions and ethnicities became accustomed to "square meals" served on divided trays. Meat and potatoes washed down with a tall glass of milk came to mean "dinner" to millions of soldiers—an expectation they carried home to their families.

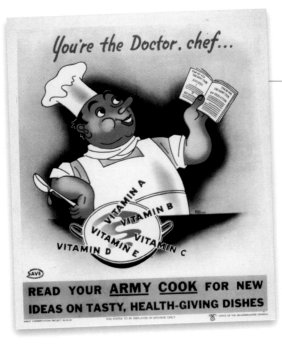

You're the Doctor Poster, ca. 1944
This poster equates cooking with medicine, emphasizing nutrition over taste.

National Archives, Records of the Office of Government Reports

Cafeteria Lines at Naval Barracks Area, Hastings, Nebraska, 1944

National Archives, Records of Naval Districts and Shore Establishments

FRESH BEEF.

I will receive proposals, till the 25th day of June, inclusive, to furnish with

FRESH BEEF,

the Troops of the U. S. Army that are, or may be, stationed at or within the vicinity of Cantonment Clinch and Pensacola, from the first of July ensuing, until the 30th of June, 1830 ; inclusive. The **BEEF** will be required to be delivered to the Troops on two days in each week, or oftener, as may be, (the days to be designated) in such quantity as may be requisite for their rations on each day. And I deem it necessary to apprize those who may offer to contract for this supply, that no beef, but the best that the Market can afford will be received, and particular attention must be paid to the butchering thereof.—A rigid inspection of it will be required.

Unquestionable and ample security will be required, for the faithful performance of the contract.

Persons offering to contract for this supply, will deposit in the Post Office at Pensacola, their proposals in writing, sealed and endorsed, "Proposals for furnishing Fresh Beef," stating in a single bid, the rate per pound, for which they will supply.

A. W. THORNTON,

Lieut. A. C. S.

Pensacola, 11th June, 1829.

In CONVENTION for the STATE of *Pennsylvania.*

FRIDAY, AUGUST 9, 1776.

On Motion, *Ordered,*

THAT Two thousand Copies of the Particulars of the Rations allowed for the FLYING CAMP, be printed and distributed among the Men.

Extract from the Minutes,

JOHN MORRIS, jun. *Secretary.*

The RATION *for each Man, as copied from the Minutes of the Honourable the* Continental CONGRESS, *is as follows,*

One Pound of Beef, or Three Quarters of a Pound of Pork, or One Pound of Salt Fish, *per* Day.

One Pound of Bread or Flour *per* Day.

Three Pints of Peas or Beans *per* Week, or Vegetables equivalent at One Dollar *per* Bushel for Peas or Beans.

One Pint of Milk *per* Man *per* Day, or at the Rate of $\frac{1}{72}$ of a Dollar.

One Half-pint of Rice, or One Pint of Indian Meal, *per* Man *per* Week.

One Quart of Spruce Beer, or Cyder, *per* Man *per* Day, or Nine Gallons of Molasses *per* Company of 100 Men *per* Week.

Three Pounds of Candles to 100 Men *per* Week, for Guards.

Twenty-four Pounds of Soft or Eight Pounds of Hard Soap for 100 Men *per* Week.

Flying Camp Rations Broadside, 1776
The Revolutionary War rations promoted in this broadside included one pint a day of spruce beer, a drink made from spruce tips and molasses thought to prevent scurvy. For colonists not fully motivated by cries of "Freedom," the promise of generous rations was a major incentive to enlist.

National Archives, Records of the Veterans Administration

Fresh Beef Broadside, 1829
Providing fresh beef to the battle-weary was a complicated endeavor. During the Revolutionary War, emaciated cattle that had been driven directly to the camps were slaughtered because there wasn't enough fodder to keep them alive. Beginning in 1827, the Army tried outsourcing its beef supply.

National Archives, Records of the Office of the Quartermaster General

 TABLE 5 | 83

World War II Poster, 1944
In 1941, *LIFE* magazine proclaimed, "Army appetites are the best fed in history." Indeed, World War II–era soldiers gained an average of 10–20 pounds during their tours of duty. Little wonder then that cooks were encouraged to "use leftovers" to help come up with the 5,000 calories a day allotted to each soldier.

National Archives, Records of the Office of Government Reports

Wanna Keep 'Em Healthy? 1944
The World War I motto "Food Will Win the War" should have been replaced by "Vitamins Will Win the War," according to World War II–era nutritionists. The newly vitamin-conscious dieticians emphasized fruits and vegetables and admonished military chefs not to overcook them.

National Archives, Records of the Office of Government Reports

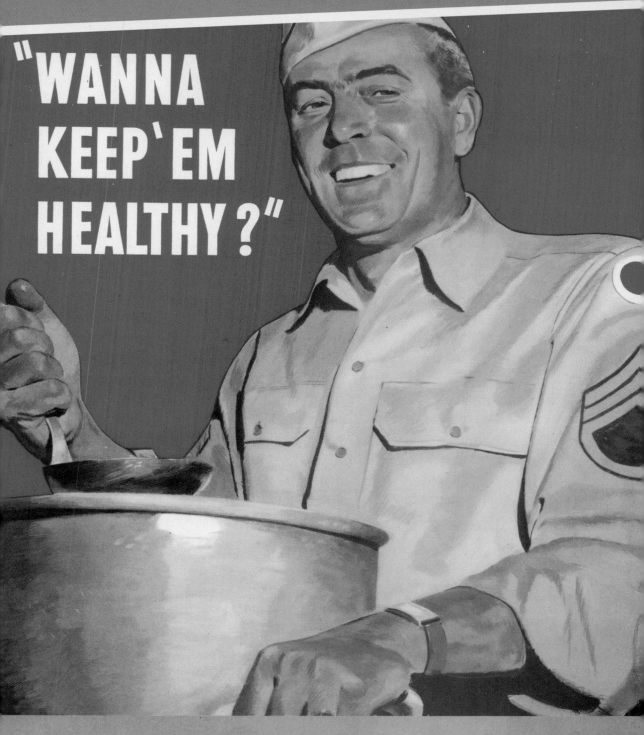

"WANNA KEEP`EM HEALTHY ?"

OVERCOOKING **DESTROYS VITAMINS !**

READING, WRITING, AND RIGATONI

Uncle Sam has touched more taste buds through the school lunch program than any other effort.

The first government support of school lunches came in the form of donated surplus commodities. This sat much better with the Depression-era public than the USDA's earlier method of disposal: plowing up crops and killing livestock. School lunch started as a child welfare program. During World War II, it became a matter of national security; malnourished children did not grow up to be good soldiers.

Approximately 7.1 million children participated in the National School Lunch Program in its first year 1946-7. Under the USDA, the program's dual goals of feeding hungry children nutritious food and supporting farmers have sometimes conflicted. Passionate public outcry has met attempts to eliminate or cut program costs. The school lunch program is one of the most popular social welfare programs in our nation's history.

Lunch Hour at the Raphael Weill Public School, San Francisco, California, 1942

National Archives, Records of the War Relocation Authority

Every Child Needs a Good School Lunch, 1944
Before the beginning of the nationwide School Lunch Program, the Government helped to support community-based programs.

National Archives, Records of Naval Districts and Shore Establishments

EVERY CHILD
NEEDS
A GOOD SCHOOL LUNCH

THE WAR FOOD ADMINISTRATION WILL HELP YOUR COMMUNITY START A
SCHOOL LUNCH PROGRAM

THE PRESIDENTIAL PALATE

". . . for the past month I have been getting sweetbreads about six times a week. I am getting to the point where my stomach positively rebels and this does not help my relations with foreign powers. I bit two of them today." —President Franklin D. Roosevelt

President Roosevelt notwithstanding, the food preferences of U.S. Presidents were generally accommodated while they were living in the White House. The contents of the President's refrigerator have long been a source of fascination for the American people. While most don't change eating habits each inaugural season, some do adopt Presidential favorites. Countless citizens have written to the White House requesting recipes.

The tastes of Presidents have ranged from the simple to the gourmet. They have hired or inherited cooks with experience ranging from world-class chef to army quartermaster. Regardless of the President's tastes, "what's cooking" at the White House is a popular and well-documented subject.

President Nixon's Last Meal at the White House, 1974

National Archives, Richard Nixon Presidential Library and Museum

President Reagan at a Meeting in the Cabinet Room, 1981
"You can tell a lot about a fellow's character by whether he picks out all of one color or just grabs a handful."
—President Ronald Reagan

National Archives, Ronald Reagan Presidential Library and Museum

BARBECUE DIPLOMACY

President Lyndon B. Johnson's first State Dinner was a Texas-style barbecue for 300. The pinto beans, barbecued spare ribs, and coleslaw were served on paper plates, buffet style—in stark contrast to the formal, elegant affairs staged by his predecessors, the Kennedys. The Johnsons hosted so many of these casual events that the term "barbecue diplomacy" was coined. Many Americans tried their first chile con queso or threw "Tex-Mex"–themed parties while Johnson was in the White House.

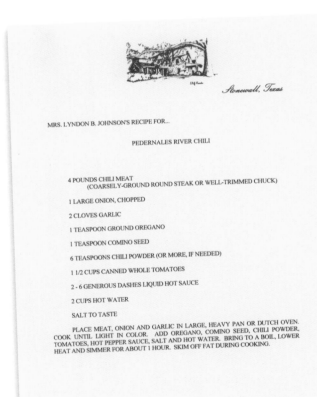

Stonewall, Texas

MRS. LYNDON B. JOHNSON'S RECIPE FOR...

PEDERNALES RIVER CHILI

4 POUNDS CHILI MEAT
(COARSELY-GROUND ROUND STEAK OR WELL-TRIMMED CHUCK)

1 LARGE ONION, CHOPPED

2 CLOVES GARLIC

1 TEASPOON GROUND OREGANO

1 TEASPOON COMINO SEED

6 TEASPOONS CHILI POWDER (OR MORE, IF NEEDED)

1 1/2 CUPS CANNED WHOLE TOMATOES

2 - 6 GENEROUS DASHES LIQUID HOT SAUCE

2 CUPS HOT WATER

SALT TO TASTE

PLACE MEAT, ONION AND GARLIC IN LARGE, HEAVY PAN OR DUTCH OVEN. COOK UNTIL LIGHT IN COLOR. ADD OREGANO, COMINO SEED, CHILI POWDER, TOMATOES, HOT PEPPER SAUCE, SALT AND HOT WATER. BRING TO A BOIL, LOWER HEAT AND SIMMER FOR ABOUT 1 HOUR. SKIM OFF FAT DURING COOKING.

Pedernales River Chili Recipe, ca. 1963–69
To accommodate recipe requests, Lady Bird Johnson had copies of LBJ's Pedernales River Chili recipe printed. She claimed they were "almost as popular as the government pamphlet on the care and feeding of children."

National Archives,
Lyndon Baines Johnson Presidential Library and Museum

President Johnson at a Barbecue for the Latin American Ambassadors, 1967

National Archives,
Lyndon Baines Johnson
Presidential Library and Museum

PEACH COBBLER AND PETIT FOURS

State Dinners reflect the tastes and preferences of their hosts. Jacqueline Kennedy ushered in an era of glamour and elegance. French food was *de rigueur*—as evidenced by the menu to the left. Rosalynn Carter, on the other hand, tried to make State Dinners less elitist and more down-home. Menus like the one on the right feature simple dishes with a Southern influence. Many Americans sampled grits for the first time when President Jimmy Carter was in office.

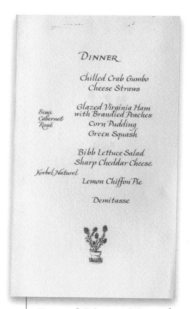

Formal Dinner Menu for Chancellor Helmut Schmidt of West Germany, 1977

National Archives, Jimmy Carter Presidential Library and Museum

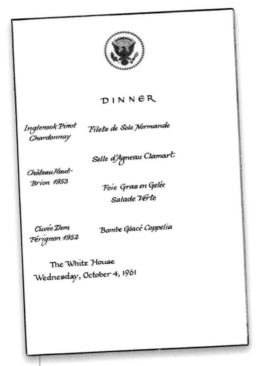

Dinner Menu from the Kennedys' State Dinner for President Abboud of the Republic of the Sudan, 1961

National Archives, John F. Kennedy Presidential Library and Museum

Dinner in Honor of the Minister of State for Cultural Affairs of France, 1962

National Archives, John F. Kennedy Presidential Library and Museum

EXACTING RECIPES FOR SIMPLE FOODS

President Dwight D. Eisenhower's vegetable soup recipe doesn't skimp on details, including directions for the disposal of leftover meat scraps—give them to your dogs or your neighbor's chickens. Eisenhower began cooking as a boy. As a young army officer, he took special interest in the feeding of his troops. Although he worked to become a first-class cook, he didn't like what he called "hifalutin gourmet stuff." Many people wrote to request his recipes.

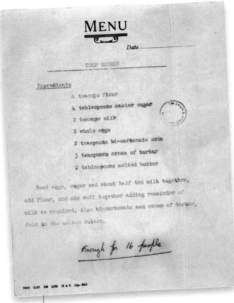

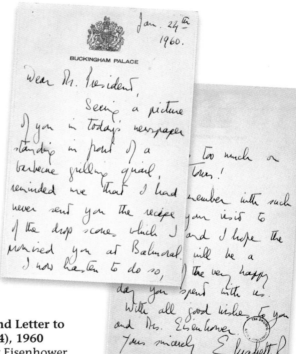

Queen Elizabeth II's Scone Recipe and Letter to President Eisenhower, (pages 1 and 4), 1960
A photo in the newspaper of President Eisenhower barbequing quail reminded Queen Elizabeth II to write this note. She included her recipe for scones, which she had promised him during his visit to Balmoral.

National Archives, Dwight D. Eisenhower Presidential Library and Museum

President Eisenhower and Former President Hoover Grill Steaks at Aksel Nielsen's Ranch near Fraser, Colorado, on September 1, 1954.

National Archives, Dwight D. Eisenhower Presidential Library and Museum

Conclusion

Food is our national pastime, our hobby, our obsession, our entertainment, and of course, our sustenance. We make choices about what to eat many times each day, often unaware how our government shapes and influences those choices.

By exploring the remarkable food records in the exhibition "What's Cooking, Uncle Sam?" and in this accompanying catalog, we learn that the U.S. Government's role in protecting us from unsafe foods dates back to the Industrial Age of the 1880s. We begin to understand the vital links between our diet and changing agricultural and industrial processes. We learn of the importance of government-sponsored research, how our knowledge of nutrition has expanded, and how our eating habits have been influenced by world events. We discover how our concerns about food have evolved over time, and we realize they are still evolving.

The subject of food has always occupied Americans and their government and it likely always will. As we continue our exploration, it is here, in the treasure trove of records held in trust for the American people at the National Archives, that we find this fascinating story of our ever-changing relationship with food.